Memories of Maiden Bradley

CHANGES IN THE LIFE OF A WILTSHIRE VILLAGE BETWEEN THE WARS

Don Newbury
27/ 8/ 2004

Don Newbury

First published in the United Kingdom in 2004 for Maiden Bradley Historical Association by The Hobnob Press, PO Box 1838, East Knoyle, Salisbury SP3 6FA

British Library Cataloguing in Publication Data
A catalogue record for this book is available from the British Library.

ISBN 0-946418-25-X

Typeset in 11/15 pt Scala
Typesetting and origination by John Chandler
Printed in Great Britain by Salisbury Printing Company Ltd, Salisbury

This book has been sponsored by Maiden Bradley Historical Association in accordance with its objectives. The Maiden Bradley Village Shop has given valuable assistance with the selling of this book and their contribution is gratefully acknowledged. So too is the useful promotion provided by Jim Downes on his Maiden Bradley website.

Picture credits. Where possible original prints have been used from the Author's collection. The Historical Association are grateful to Eileen Seal, Marilyn Doel, Reg Prowse, Chris Oliver, Derek Stevens and Colin Dowson for the use of prints from their collections. The original photographers are not always known but include John Scanes, John Dilworth, Dr. Pope Bartlett and Basil Leather. The cover paintings are by Susan Hanson and were bequeathed to All Saints' Church by her son Christopher Hanson. *Front cover:* Chip Cottage; *Back cover:* Maiden Bradley Priory. Both reproduced by permission of the Vicar and Churchwarden.

Foreword by John Seymour, Duke of Somerset

L ET ME WELCOME YOU to this fascinating book recounting two decades of the history of the small Wiltshire village where I have spent so much of my life. Don Newbury will be one of the few who can still remember all the changes of the twenties, and he is to be congratulated for making such an effort to transcribe them on to paper.

As Don writes, this period in the history of the village is intimately interwoven with the history of the Bradley Estate, owned by my family, and thus it is of great interest to read of personalities and events that influenced the running of the business and it helps to answer the recurring question of 'why did they do that?'.

Some of you will recall parts of his story, and many more will enjoy the old photographs and reminiscences, but everyone will be grateful for this insight to a world less than a lifetime away, but now vanished for ever.

Bradley House
Maiden Bradley
March 2004

Maiden Bradley school children Group 3 with the Author third from the left at the back, c. 1921.

The Author cutting his 90th birthday cake.

M AIDEN BRADLEY, in common with other villages of the time, was a flourishing and healthy community with a well-filled school. There was a police station with a resident policeman, shop, post office, blacksmith's shop, chimney sweep, bakery, carpenter and wheelwright's business, undertaker and a pub. There were two milk retailers and two coal and wood merchants. There was All Saints' Church and the Congregational Chapel, a village hall, reading room, nurse, and a carrier's business with horse transport to Frome market and with pony and traps for hire on special occasions.

I grew up in these times and now hope to give you an insight into how we lived in the village of Maiden Bradley in the early part of the twentieth century.

Don Newbury
January 2004

The Early 1920s

MAIDEN BRADLEY was a well maintained estate; all the cottages, farms and woodlands were owned by the Duke of Somerset as well as those in Gare Hill and Witham Friary.

Most of the houses in the village had creeper or ivy growing on the walls which completely covered many of them. It was the wish of Susan Duchess that the creeper was kept trimmed throughout the year (around the windows and under the eaves) and under no circumstances was it to be destroyed. The trimming was the responsibility of the householder, with the exception of the elderly whose houses were kept trimmed by the estate workers.

All the houses were kept in good repair by the estate and regularly painted. The front and back doors were painted dark brown (known as 'estate brown'), the windows were brown and white and the rest of the wood was painted dark brown.

In the early 1920s there were only about six houses with flush toilets, the remainder had a bucket or vault toilet in a little wooden shed in the garden, some being as far as forty yards from the house. The only premises connected to the main (estate) sewer were the nurse's house, the village hall, the school, the pub, the land agent's house and Bradley House; it was quite a number of years before more houses were connected. From Bradley House the main sewer went on down Kingston Lane to the sewage works which always seemed to keep going without any problems. It was some thirty or forty years before the Rank and Frome Road were on the main sewer.

Maiden Bradley had a very efficient water supply installed by the estate in 1896. There was a plentiful supply of water from the springs at Dunkerton which ran down to the mill, where a water wheel drove the pumps to force the water up (one mile) to the reservoir at Mapperton Hill. From here gravity took it down to the village where a good pressure was maintained. There was always a plumber employed by the estate to maintain the pumps and do any repairs necessary. One of the duties of the plumber was to visit the pumps at the Mill daily, including Sundays, to inspect and oil the machinery.

The Duke of Somerset's agent and the Clerk of Works lived in the village, and in the estate office two clerks were employed full-time and usually kept very busy. The Head Forester also lived in the village. Every morning he could be seen going down to the estate office at 9 am where he would have a meeting with the Land Agent.

A Wiltshire County Council roadman lived in the village and his Saturday mornings were always spent cleaning it up. We also had a bakery renowned for its lardy cakes and buns as well as bread. These were delivered around the village daily by the baker using a covered handcart.

The School

T HE SCHOOL had (in 1921/22) approximately 60 pupils – split into three classrooms. The Headmaster was John Scanes who taught the older children in the Big Room; Mrs. Ludlow taught the middle group in one of the smaller rooms and Miss Nellie Gillanders used another classroom for the infants. Mrs. Scanes worked part-time and was able to take over when needed.

The school bell was rung each school day for five minutes from 8.55 to 9 am. and again for the afternoon session from 1.25 to 1.30 pm – the bell could be heard from all over the village.

No transport was provided in those days, the children from outlying districts all had to walk to school, even the children just starting school at the age of five. Children came in to school from Rodmead, Newmead, Yarnfield, Mill Cottages, parts of Norton Ferris, Baycliff, Bricefield and sometimes St. Algars. Quite often the children would arrive at school wet through after walking in on a wet morning. In winter time the children that had a long journey home were allowed to leave 15 minutes earlier to (hopefully) get home in the daylight.

The children that walked to school from the outlying areas brought their own lunch of sandwiches and a bottle of tea which they ate in the Big Room. In the winter a bath of water was put on the top of the stove and on arrival the bottles of tea were stood in the bath to keep them warm until lunchtime to enable the children to have a hot drink with their sandwiches.

The Rev. A.J. Wilcox, Vicar of Maiden Bradley
1920 with village school teachers.
Miss N. Gillanders, Mrs. Scanes, Mrs. L. Ludlow,
Photograph by Mr. John Scanes, Headmaster.

At the school we had two play-yards divided off by a 6 ft wall, one for the girls and infants and the other for the boys. There were flush toilets at the far side of the yard. The school was heated by combustion stoves in each room.

John Scanes was a very good teacher, very strict and very thorough. He was not interested in sport and the only recreation that the children had were 15 minute breaks in the morning and afternoon sessions which were spent in the play yard. The school gardens were cultivated and kept tidy by the older boys and usually produced some good crops. Mr. Scanes was a strict believer in discipline and would never hesitate to give the boys a good old fashioned 'clip around the ear'. Mr. Scanes was a big man, over 6 ft tall and weighing about 16 stone and when he clouted you, you knew you had been clouted; he was also very handy with the cane which was used quite often. He kept the cane behind a big map of the world which was hanging on the wall behind his desk and when he got out of his chair and reached up under the map for his cane you knew he meant business.

On winter evenings Mr. Scanes would hold evening classes for some of the older children who wished to improve their education. Some of the pupils did well and in later years graduated into shrewd and successful businessmen.

Mr. Scanes excelled in photography, many of his photos of the village are still in existence.

He had a motorcycle combination (called a James) and thought nothing of packing up school on a Friday afternoon and going off to Ide, near Exeter (where he had relatives and property which he visited quite often) for the weekend, never failing to be back on Monday morning. He would wear a leather jacket, a fur-lined leather helmet and a pair of goggles. Mrs. Scanes would be in the sidecar well wrapped up complete with her helmet and goggles and a rug around her legs. The bike had acetylene lighting and I often wondered how he managed journeys with such poor lighting.

On his retirement in the early 1920s Mr. Scanes moved back to Ide. He then had time to do more work for the Devizes Museum where some of his books and other work can still be seen.

The Post Office

T HE POST OFFICE incorporated a telephone exchange and a sorting office for the mail. In addition to the Maiden Bradley phones, the Horningsham subscribers (including Longleat House) were connected to the Bradley exchange and therefore had Maiden Bradley telephone numbers. Kingston Deverill and parts of Kilmington were also on the Maiden Bradley exchange.

The postmaster and his wife operated the exchange 24 hours a day but as years passed and more 'phones were connected full-time telephone operators were employed.

In the early 1920s the postal address was 'Maiden Bradley, Bath, Somerset' but it was changed to 'Maiden Bradley, Frome, Somerset' and from then onwards all the mail was handled by Frome Post Office. Mail was brought out from there at 6 am each morning by bicycle and was sorted at Bradley Post Office for delivery by the postmen on bikes around the village and also to the Deverills, Kilmington, Gare Hill and Witham Friary. Four full-time postmen were employed and based at Maiden Bradley.

The postman that delivered the mail around the village and all the outlying farms, including Rodmead and Newmead, was Ernie Newbury. He had only one arm (having been wounded in World War I) but in spite of this he was quite capable of carrying a heavy bag of mail and doing an efficient job. Charlie Newbury delivered down through the Deverills and finished at Longbridge. He would wait there at the Post Office until 4 pm when he would pick up any mail for Maiden Bradley district and return with it.

George Howell, another postman, would do the Kilmington and Norton Ferris round again returning to Maiden Bradley at 4 pm with mail from Kilmington Post Office. Jim Hacker did the Gare Hill and Witham Friary round for many years on foot, covering sometimes more than 14 miles a day. He rented an allotment at Witham Friary upon which he had a little shed erected where he could go and have his lunch or shelter when it rained. During his waiting time at Witham he would cultivate the allotment and grow lots of vegetables. After some years Mr. Hacker learned to ride a bicycle which proved to be very helpful.

The departure of the mail at 8 pm from the Old Post Office. A Holbrook, G Howell, F Newbury, C Newbury and J Hacker.

The postmaster was Albert Griffen but his wife did most of the work in the post office as he worked at the local blacksmith's shop full-time. The post box was cleared nightly at 7.50 pm when a post office van would come out from Frome. People could set their watches by this van which always left Bradley precisely at 8 pm. The Post Office only sold stationery, stamps and postal orders and paid out pensions.

The Shop

THE VILLAGE SHOP (now the Manor House) was a branch of Walton's Departmental Store of Mere. The shop was entered by the main entrance in Church Street – up the steps, through the front door into the hall where you turned right to the Drapery department and left into the Grocery department.

Nearly everything could be bought at Walton's, if it was not in stock at the Maiden Bradley branch they would order it from Mere and it would be sent the next day on approval.

I remember when I left school at the age of 14 I said to my mother 'Now that I shall be starting work I will need some trousers and hob-nailed boots' – all boys wore short trousers to school, long trousers were never worn until you left school. Mother said that I had better go down to the shop and order some. I went to the shop and told the manager I wanted some long trousers and hob-nailed boots. He measured me and asked me the size of the boots and sure enough the next day three pairs of trousers and three pairs of boots were delivered on approval at our house so I was able to start work in my new boots and trousers.

Walton's were able to supply anything from their grocery, drapery, footwear, ironmongery, furniture, ladies' fashions or gents' outfitters departments. They even had a cabinet-making shop and would make high-class furniture to order.

Maiden Bradley Football Team 1920
Back Row (left to right) Jess Wilkins, Percy Doel, Bert Wilkins, Joe Curtis, Len Smart, Basil Leather, Matt Flower, Arthur Smith, Harry May
Second Row Fred Stone, Bert Newbury, Jack Seal, Arthur Wilson, Edgar Howell
Front Row Ben Crees, Bill Snook

They kept two delivery vans at the Maiden Bradley premises. They were both Ford Model T, 10 cwt vans, painted green with gold lettering – always looking very smart and in first class condition. These vans were in daily use for deliveries to Witham Friary, Horningsham, Kilmington and parts of the Deverills. The shop manager would go around these villages, taking orders, in his car (an old Bull Nosed Morris). The shop also did a very good trade around the district selling pig and poultry foods – the vans usually had a full load on board when they started their rounds.

At Maiden Bradley Walton's had a slaughter house in which pigs were killed on Tuesdays. A plentiful supply of bacon and ham and everything that came from a pig was always on sale at the shop. The slaughterman was a local man who also did part-time van driving. There were two full-time men working in the grocery department as well as two assistants in the drapery department and one person in the office. One van driver and two bakers were also kept busy. Quite often the shop would employ one or two school leavers for weighing up sugar and other groceries that arrived in bulk.

Walton's were noted for selling very good quality goods and even the Duke of Somerset would buy his suits from their gents' outfitters department in Mere.

The Pub – The Somerset Arms

T HE LANDLORD OF THE PUB was A.G. (George) Locke who, in addition to running the pub had quite a few sidelines.

George Locke had a farm, 'Dangell's Farm', and a milk round in the village – George Pole ran the farm and brought milk around the village every morning in a horse drawn milk float. George Locke also had a coal and wood business. Coal and wood were sold around the village in 1cwt sacks. There was quite a demand as all the houses had open fireplaces and coal and wood were used for heating and cooking – central heating was still a long way off.

Mr. Locke usually kept four or five heavy horses in the stable (now the skittle alley) which were used for contracting; sometimes hauling timber out of the woods, other times on hire to the Wiltshire County Council to work with the gangs of men repairing the roads. George also acted as a buying agent for the Writhlington Colliery at Radstock. He would buy standing timber from the Maiden Bradley Estate and get the trees cut down. His horses would then haul them out of the wood and take them to the top of Grace's Hill (Chip Cottage) where they were stacked by the side of a static crane. The wood was then fetched by Writhlington Colliery's own transport (a big steam lorry) and used as pit props.

George Locke had the first lorry in the district, a Ford Model T (one tonner) which he used for fetching coal from the Radstock pits, for wood hauling and for fetching beer from the breweries at Frome.

After World War I the village football team was formed and horse transport was used to take the team to the away matches until George Locke offered the use of his lorry. Some steps were made to get up into the lorry where the passengers sat on forms and where there was no protection from the weather. The footballers used the lorry for a few years until Basil Leather had his first bus in 1923.

George Locke seemed to have a good eye for business. He bought a new car which was another Ford – a four-seater which he used for taxi work. He would allow anyone to borrow it for a modest fee provided they could drive. There was a fellow in the village who would often borrow it to take a load of lads to Frome or Warminster to the pictures – quite a good, cheap evening out.

George employed four full-time men and quite often three or four part-time. One man was always working at the pub. There were no floor coverings in the bar or the lounge just flagstones which were washed every day. Harry Viney could be seen most days washing down the front steps with his mop and bucket and we kids would often stand and watch him spinning the mop to get the water out.

The Blacksmith's Shop and Wheelwright's & Carpenter's Business

DURING THE WAR YEARS and on into the early 1920s these businesses were run by Mr. H. J. Baker who lived at Fountain View in Church Street. Three blacksmiths were employed and always appeared to be kept busy shoeing horses and repairing the farm machinery.

All the farms used heavy horses for the work on the farms, ploughing, sowing seed, haymaking, harvesting and all general farm work, some farms had as many as ten horses as well as one or two hunters. The blacksmiths were kept busy making the shoes as well as having to shoe all these horses. It was a common sight to go up into the yard and see as many as half a dozen horses tied up and waiting to be shod.

As kids we were fascinated to go up into the yard and look over the half door and watch the sparks as the shoes were being made. The sound of the hammer on the anvil could be heard all over the village. There were always lots of farm implements lined up in the yard awaiting repair, particularly at mowing and harvesting time – the busiest times of the year. The shoeing iron was delivered in long bars from Bristol and stored in racks before being made into shoes.

The carpentry and wheelwright business was run from premises in High Street (a bungalow now occupies the site). Carts and wagons were built and repaired in the carpenter's shop as well as coaches; the Duke of Somerset's carriages were often taken in for maintenance and repairs. There was a sawmill on which timber was cut into board for use when required. Two men worked at these premises and often had to do overtime to keep up with the work.

Villagers could go along to the carpenter's shop and buy any paint they needed and in any colour, as the paint was mixed on the premises while one waited. Mr. Baker also had an undertaker's business and did most of the local work. All the coffins were made at the carpenter's shop.

The Village Garage

THE GARAGE BEGAN in the early 1920s when Alfred Griffen (son of the postmaster) bought one of the ex-army huts that were being dismantled from the army camp at Sutton Veny. He erected it at the top of his father's garden by the side of the track leading into the estate yard and it was approached through a gate leading off the Bruton road. The garage has stood the test of time and is still standing after many years of use.

The garage kept open most evenings and was a focal point for the village. If you went up to the garage on a winter evening (perhaps to buy a battery for your flashlamp or a pair of brake blocks for your bike) it was highly probable that you would stay and have a yarn with Alf Griffen. He always kept a big stove red hot which made his customers reluctant to want to go out in the cold – some people would make an excuse to go to the garage just to have a good warm up!

In the early days there was very little trade done in the repair of motor cars or motorbikes but as the years passed it improved as motor cars became more popular. Soon there was enough work for Alf's brother Max to go into partnership with him. They were now selling new bikes as well as doing lots of cycle repairs. They bought an old car and started hiring it out and always kept an assortment of cycle spares as well as a few motor spares.

There were still only a few people in the village that had cars when Griffens started to sell petrol. It was sold in two-gallon cans and soon most of the villagers were buying their petrol there. A good trade was done selling paraffin, as most people in the village had oil lamps and some had oil stoves for cooking.

Griffens were well established in business when Alf Griffen branched out into photography. He took lots of photos of the village which can still be seen today.

After getting the business established the whole of the Griffen family decided to emigrate. In 1924 they packed up and went to Australia where they took over a relative's garage business which they built up into a large profitable concern. One of the younger members of the family (Ivor) joined the Australian army and fought in World War II, at which time he was able to visit Maiden Bradley and look up some of his old chums.

The Village Carrier, Coal & Wood Merchant, Milk Retailer and Contractor

T HE CARRIER'S BUSINESS entailed running a regular service to Frome on Wednesdays with a horse-drawn covered van which could carry ten passengers. This was the only means the village people had of getting to town to do shopping; it was a very useful service and was usually well patronised. The business was run by Mr. Edward Doman who also had a coal and wood business as well as being a milk retailer.

The milk was produced at Laurel Farm and taken to Mr. Doman's house at 55 The Rank each day by the farm manager, Mr. Trimby, where people would go with their cans or jugs to fetch their milk.

Mr. Doman kept five horses and a pony, the horses were used for timber work and for fetching coal from the pits at Radstock and retailing it around the district. The Wiltshire County Council also hired the horses for work on the roads – they were usually kept busy.

Harold White and Don Newbury having just loaded Basil Leather's
timber carriage in Bradley woods.
Picture taken by Basil Leather

Basil Leather started work for Mr. Doman when he was demobbed from the army after World War I. Most of his time was taken up with going to Radstock to collect coal with a horse and wagon; this was a hard day's work for the horse and also the driver (14 miles each way). An early start had to be made for this job – usually between 3 and 5 am and on arrival at the coal pit the horse was 'hitched out' and put into the stable with a good feed and a drink of water. It could have a well-earned rest while the wagon was being loaded before making the return journey to Maiden Bradley.

On many occasions when they were doing the Radstock trip Mr. Doman would come over to the school during playtime and ask me to take a trace horse down to the bottom of Bradley Hill to await the wagon from Radstock and help him up the hill. The horse that had hauled the loaded wagon from Radstock would be very tired and a bit of help for the last couple of miles was always welcome.

A bus now started running from Wincanton to Frome on Wednesdays and Saturdays, operated by Woodcocks Wincanton Motor Services. This proved to be very useful for people to shop in Frome and was a much quicker and more comfortable journey than the horse-drawn van. In addition to shopping trips, Woodcocks also ran a late evening service to the 'pictures' which was always very crowded.

Perhaps the fact that the bus would take all his trade prompted Mr. Doman to think of retirement. Anyway it was not very long before it was known in the village that Mr. Doman was retiring and Basil Leather was taking over. After some negotiations with the Estate Basil Leather took over the carriers' business and the firewood, coal and contracting businesses together with the yard, stables, coach houses, cart sheds and all other sheds as well as two fields, three horses and a pony.

The farm was taken over by Mr. Bert Smith who set up a milk round in the village. He delivered in the morning and again in the afternoon – it was much appreciated by the villagers having milk delivered to the door.

Basil Leather knew when he took on the business that he would have to turn over to motor transport to be able to compete with the Wincanton bus. In 1923 he bought his first motor vehicle which was a dual-purpose lorry–bus – a Model T Ford 1 tonner. As a bus it carried fourteen passengers and as a lorry it would carry a ton in weight. Basil could now compete with the bus that came

The first motor vehicle to be owned by B.C. Leather in 1923. A Model T Ford dual purpose vehicle which could carry 14 passengers or, when used as a lorry, would carry one ton. Taken on Maiden Bradley Crossroads by Mr. John Scanes who set his camera up on the Knapp. Note the School House covered with creeper and the flagpole in the background. Shown in the picture are (left to right) O. Randall, Don Newbury and Basil Leather.

through the village and could also fetch coal back from Radstock much quicker than by horse transport. To convert the bus to a lorry took no more than ten minutes – the bus section being lifted up by pulley blocks from a beam in the garage.

Village people were very supportive of Basil's efforts and soon he had to buy another vehicle to cope with the extra work. This time he bought a fourteen-seater charabanc, a Chevrolet, which was a much improved vehicle over the Ford.

To earn a little extra revenue when running the service into town on Wednesdays, Basil Leather would do shopping for the village people and charge them tuppence or threepence for his trouble. People appreciated the fact that they could have their shopping done without having to spend a day in town.

The Village Hall

THE VILLAGE HALL had been used during World War I as a military hospital and after it had been handed back it was used for social events. A 'men's club' was formed and on many nights each week the hall was used for recreation such as billiards, skittles, cards and darts, etc.

After a few years the club was transferred to the Reading Room (a cottage on the opposite side of the road) and the hall could now be used for whist drives, dances and concerts. A local concert party was started giving performances and holding social evenings during the winter months. A string orchestra was formed with village people, consisting of five violins, a cello, double bass and piano. They put on concerts from jazz to dance and classical music, which were very much enjoyed by, usually, a hall full of people.

The Duke and Duchess of Somerset would attend these concerts. The chauffeur would arrive (in full uniform) a few minutes before the concert began with the Duke and Duchess wearing evening dress. They would sit in the front row of seats in two luxury armchairs that had been brought from Bradley House. The seating was arranged by the estate carpenters during the day and quite often the front of the stage was adorned with pot plants and flowers from the greenhouses. When the concert ended the chauffeur was on hand to usher the Duke and Duchess out to their waiting car before the rest of the people were allowed to leave.

The Duke of Somerset's chauffeur, 'Mac' Bertie Macleod with the 1925 Armstrong Siddeley 18 Mk2.

It was called the Village Hall but of course was owned and run, as well as being maintained, by the Estate. The chairman of the committee was always the Agent and the secretary was the Clerk of Works, who was in charge of the lettings. The hall could boast a full set of china with eighty cups and saucers and all the plates and dishes required for a complete meal. When hiring the Hall you were asked if you needed the use of the china (for which you paid extra). The china would be counted out to you by the Secretary who would count it back in after the event – any breakages had to be paid for. There were eighty wooden chairs and two wooden arm chairs as well as plenty of whist tables.

The Hall garden (which is now the car park) was used by the estate Forestry Department as a nursery for growing young trees which, when large enough, were planted out in the woods. The nursery was kept in immaculate condition (together with the hedges surrounding the hall) by George Edwards, one of the estate workmen.

The lighting in the hall was provided by acetylene gas. A number of lights hung from the ceiling as well as lights on brackets over all the interior doors, all the cloakrooms were well lit as was the porch, and an outside light each side of the entrance porch showed people up the steps. The lighting was the responsibility of the estate plumber, who always had to be on duty at all winter events when lighting was required. The apparatus for the lights was kept in a shed at the back of the Hall.

While in use as a military hospital three baths were installed in the hall. One was in what is now the kitchen, one in the ladies cloakroom and the other in the gents cloakroom and a heating apparatus was installed in one of the buildings at the rear. After the war the baths proved to be useful to the village as only about six houses had bathrooms. People were able to take a towel and go to the hall on a Saturday and have a bath for fourpence. Mr. Doel, the caretaker, would light up a fire in the heating apparatus in the early morning so that plenty of hot water was available to keep the three baths going all day. For a few years this proved to be a very popular alternative to heating up kettles

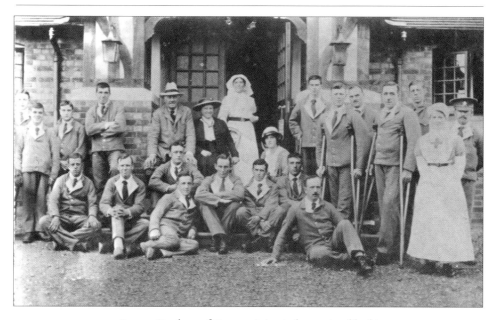

Susan, Duchess of Somerset (seated, wearing black)
with wounded soldiers when the Village Hall was used
as a hospital during the World War I.
Nurse Gillanders wearing Red Cross uniform (front row, right)
was later to become the village Nurse, a post she held for many years

of water and having a bath in the old galvanised tub in front of the fire after the rest of the family had gone to bed.

The Village Nurse – Miss Mary Gillanders

THE NURSE lived at the Surgery in High Street (now a private house – number 71) where the doctor held a surgery on Monday and Friday evenings from 5 pm to 6.30 pm. Medicines were dispensed at the surgery during visiting hours. The usual procedure was to see the doctor during visiting hours; he would then mix up the medicines required and people went back at 7 pm to pick them up – they were left in a box in the Surgery porch. This system worked very well and appeared to satisfy the patients. The doctor was Dr. Pope Bartlett; he operated the same practice that we have to the present day. Dr. Bartlett lived at Bourton and travelled to Maiden Bradley in an old Morris two-seater car but before he had the car he had been coming by various means of transport. For a number of years he had a pony and trap which he would arrive in during the afternoon and after putting the pony in the pub stable he would go into the pub and have tea before going to surgery. After the pony days he came on a motorcycle and by the time he retired he had graduated to a Bull Nosed Morris.

Nurse Gillanders was a very good nurse and some people had more confidence in her than in the doctor. Susan Duchess of Somerset was anxious to have a well qualified nurse in the village so she had paid all her expenses to go to a leading hospital in London for training. After she qualified (specialising in child care) she came back to the village to continue her nursing career.

Jack Seal complete with bowler hat, with the horse and trap ready to take Nurse Gillanders to her next appointment. Picture taken in the Duke of Somerset's Stable Yard (1923)

In addition to being the village nurse, she made visits to Gare Hill, Witham Friary and any other farms or properties on the Duke's estate. The Duke would provide transport for any calls that were beyond walking distance. It was a common sight to see the groom (Jack Seal) setting off with the nurse in the horse and trap (complete with her little black bag) and in the winter all wrapped up in rugs.

Maiden Bradley Fountain. Note the railings, a round iron bar at the top and three strands of wire at the bottom. The platform at the front of the fountain where the horses would stand to drink was some eighteen inches above the level of the road in those days, since then the road has been made up two feet or more.
Inscription on the Fountain
Drink travellers drink of Bradley's purest rill
Which strange to say runs quite a mile uphill
Then to your panting steed let all attend
An honest horse is truly man's best friend

The Fountain

C RYSTAL CLEAR WATER flowed out of the fox's head at all times, day and night. In the 1920s the fountain was used quite a lot – it provided a welcome drink for the many horses that travelled through the village. There were two breweries in Frome which both relied on horses to deliver their stocks to the pubs in the district, sometimes twice a week. They came through the village with loaded drays on route to pubs in the Maiden Bradley, Kilmington, Stourton, Mere, Zeals and Bourton area, and they always stopped at Bradley for a drink and a rest at the fountain.

A copper cup on a copper chain hung from a hook near the fox's head and often cyclists and other travellers would stop and have a drink when they passed. The local dogs could often be seen having a drink from the dog trough.

The fountain was always maintained in immaculate condition by the estate. It was the duty of Mr. Frank Doel, the head painter, to clean the fountain every Saturday morning and check that everything was working well.

Church Street has been resurfaced regularly since the twenties and the road is now about eighteen inches higher. It can be seen from photographs that horses had to step up with their front feet on to the tiled area of the fountain – now it is approximately twelve inches below the road.

During World War I troops from the large army camps at Longbridge Deverill and Sutton Veny would often come through the village on route marches and as the Eagle above the fountain was the German emblem they would throw stones at it. The estate had a wire mesh grill made to cover the eagle to avoid damage but in the end the estate had to remove it. It was replaced after the War.

Street Lighting

W HEN THE BLACKOUT RESTRICTIONS were lifted after World War I street lighting was introduced in Church Street and High Street.

Most of the eleven lamps were fitted to cast iron ornamental standards about eight or ten feet high, some were fitted on brackets mounted on houses. The lamps were about the same size as the gas lamps in the towns, but were of course lit by paraffin. The oil containers on the lamps were quite large and the lamps would burn all the week on one refill. The lamps were lit soon after 5 pm in the winter and put out at 10 pm.

A ladder was needed when the lamps were lit. This meant that one had to be carried down as far as the Church (where the lamp standard was opposite the gates) and up as far as Perry Farm in the High Street by Mr. H. Doel who was in charge of the lighting arrangements. At 10 pm Mr. Doel, or one of his sons, would go around the village with a long pole with a hook attachment on it; this was fixed into a ring on the burner to put the lamps out.

Mr. Doel would fill and clean all the lamps on Saturday afternoons. During the summer when the lights were not needed they were taken down and stored in the Estate yard. It was surprising the amount of light these lamps gave – very helpful to the village people who had to go out on a winter's night. This form of lighting continued until 1938 when electricity was installed in Maiden Bradley. The lamp posts and brackets were commandeered and taken down by the government for scrap during the Second World War but one remains at the Church.

The Village Policeman

I N C O M M O N with most other villages we had a village Policeman, P.C. Attwell, who kept a very wary eye on all the goings on in the village. He had very little motor traffic to contend with although he would catch the odd vehicle with only one sidelight or no rear light. Riding a bike with no lights was what he concentrated on; he used to catch quite a few of the villagers who had to appear at Warminster Police Court where the fine was usually seven shillings and six pence, some got away for five shillings.

P.C. Attwell was never troubled with vandalism in the village except for the odd prank by some of the older lads. You never knew when or where he might show up in the village and he appeared to be on duty at all times day or night. He did however have a day off sometimes and then the village was patrolled by a policeman from one of the neighbouring villages.

P.C. Attwell lived at the Police Station in the High Street (number 74). As well as using his bicycle for some of his duties he could sometimes be seen riding around on his B.S.A. motorcycle combination – he used this when he had to go to Warminster Station on Thursdays for drill.

The Church

T H E V I C A R, who lived in the Vicarage, was the Rev. Alfred J. Wilcox (a bachelor) who sometimes had a housekeeper or male servant to look after him. He held two services on Sundays at 11 am and 6.30 pm and also Sunday School in the church in the afternoons. The bells were rung for all services. For the morning services the 'Old Ringers' were on duty (these were men mostly sixty or seventy years old) who had been ringers for many years. For the evening services a team of younger lads (some learners) were on duty and they did their best to perform well and avoid criticism from the Old Boys. In addition to ringing for special services the bells were rung on Christmas morning at 6 am and always on New Year's Eve, starting at 11.30 pm with a half muffled peal till

Maiden Bradley Church Outing to Weymouth 1920
Picture taken on arrival at Weymouth.
The charabanc was 'The Forest Queen' from Gillingham driven by Tom Lawley.
Note the oil side lights and the chain driven back axle.

midnight. Then one of the ringers would dash off up into the bell chamber and remove the leather muffles from the bells so that at midnight a good peal would be rung to welcome in the New Year.

In those days there were more seats in the Church – a few more around the font as well as more over the far side. There were choir stalls with seating for approximately a dozen, there being as many as ten men and boys in the choir at most services, all wearing cassocks.

A stained glass window adorned the chancel at the back of the altar. The organ was then at the east end and was played from in the chancel. A boy was detailed to be on duty to pump the organ when it was to be played. The chiming apparatus was then where the organ is now, under the tower.

The Church was lit by oil lamps hanging on the chains where the electric lights now are. Quite a number of candles were also used. Heating was by a coke-fired apparatus. The verger was on duty to fill, clean and light the lamps and also to be in charge of the heating system. In winter it was nearly a full-time job for him to keep everything in working order. It was also his duty to climb the steps to the ringing chamber to wind up the clock every evening and to lock the Church after the services.

The bell ringers were entertained by the vicar each year at the Vicarage for a lavish Christmas party. Caterers were hired to provide a hot meal of turkey, Christmas pudding and all the trimmings plus a good selection of drinks. This tradition was kept going until the late 1930s when the war intervened.

On a Sunday in June each year a service was held at the Church at 3 pm. It was known as the Cyclists' Service, when the Bath Cycling Club (usually some sixty to eighty cyclists) would attend. After the service the vicar would provide tea on the Vicarage lawn for the whole party before they cycled back to Bath. This was a very popular event for many years.

Maiden Bradley Church Outing to Bournemouth 1921
Back Row: Dora Viney, Mrs. Viney, Miss C. Viney, Miss L. Dredge, Mrs. Dredge
Second Row: Mrs. Cleal, Miss M. Gray, Mrs. Clark, Mrs. A. White, Miss V. White
Third Row: Mrs. Coleman, Mrs. Hulance, Ethel Hulance, Mrs. (Granny) Ford, Bessie Ford,
Mrs. Minney Merritt
Fourth Row: Mrs. Reg. Miles, Bertram Miles, Mrs. Charlie Newbury, Mrs. George Howell,
Mrs. Frank Doel, Charles Doel
Fifth Row: Don Newbury, Mrs. Francis Newbury, Mrs. J. Mounty, Mrs. G. Curtis, Mrs.
Martha Newbury, Mrs. G. Snook
Front Row: Driver: Walter Higson (owner of Crown Tours, Frome), Rev. A.J. Wilcox, Miss
Amy Curtis, Miss Millie Curtis
Picture taken at Salisbury (The Canal)

Another event was the annual Church fête which was held on a Saturday in June in the Vicarage grounds. This was always very popular and attended by most of the villagers. There were the usual stalls and amusements as well as children's and adult sports. The headmaster would organise a fancy dress parade with decorated handcarts. He always had a good turnout as most of the kids in the school entered – you had to have a good excuse if you told him you did not want to join in.

Parade of decorated handcarts at Maiden Bradley Church Fête held in the vicarage grounds 1923
Left to right: Willie Doel, Perry Baker, Bill Holly, Len Waters, Les Read, Bill Newbury, Toby Dulake, Percy Snook and Don Newbury

In 1937 the fête was opened by the Emperor of Abyssinia. He was living in Bath in exile after the Italian invasion of his country. I remember him standing on a platform when opening the fete and making a speech in his native language with an interpreter standing by his side translating into English.

The Congregational Chapel

T HE CHAPEL was well patronised; a morning and evening service was held every Sunday with Sunday school in the afternoon.

Maiden Bradley shared the Pastor with Horningsham, he was the Rev. George D. Davis who took a service at Maiden Bradley every Sunday as well as one at Horningsham – alternating morning one week and evening the next. He turned up regularly every week on his bike whatever the weather. He lived at the Manse in Horningsham. The other services were taken by a preacher usually from Frome or Mere.

The big organ upstairs was used for the services and there was always a choir of as many as ten people to boost the singing. A car-load of people usually came out from Frome every Sunday to the services.

The Superintendent of the Chapel was Matthew Henry Sims (my grandfather) who was also the Sunday School teacher. He would organise the Sunday School outing each year; this was always to Stourton Tower by horse transport and sometimes it needed two or three horses and brakes to accommodate the party of children and parents.

Sports and games were held on the grass in front of the tower after which a good tea was provided and a big jar of sweets shared out between the children. The outing was always enjoyed by the whole party provided the weather was favourable.

The Reading Room

T HE READING ROOM CLUB was held in the cottage in High Street, number 67 opposite the Village Hall. It was well patronised by the men of the village and Mr. George Curtis was the very efficient secretary. You were allowed to become a member on reaching the age of 16 (provided you were sponsored by one of the Committee members). A fee of sixpence was charged for the use of the billiard board for half an hour but all the other games were free on payment of the membership fee. The billiard table and the ring and the dart boards were in the downstairs room – the rest of the games were upstairs, which included table skittles and card games.

One of the committee members was on duty every evening. There was a rota whereby each member did a week-long stint. During the winter months the Bradley club would play other clubs in the district, usually four each at billiards, draughts and cards (twelve in a team). Bradley could usually put up a good show as there were a few good players in the village; at billiards and draughts particularly they could hold their own with most of the opposition.

The game of quoits was played in the summer in the garden at the rear. A clay bed was laid out five feet square and at the other end of the garden another

Maiden Bradley Reading Room Committee – 1927
Back row L to R: Harry White, Jack Seal, Ray Newbury, Joe Curtis, Lew Newbury, George Edwards
Front Row L to R: Maurice Newbury, Charlie Seal, Basil Leather, George Curtis (Hon.
Sec.), Edgar Howell, Fred Fowler, Arthur Newbury
Picture taken at rear of Reading Room by John Dilworth (Butler to the Duke of Somerset)
who lived in Duke's Cottage, in Kingston Lane.

roughly fifteen yards away with a metal pin in the middle. This was the target at which round iron quoits were thrown with most points awarded for being nearest to the pin. A team was formed and they played in the Warminster league giving a good account of themselves for a few seasons.

A Reading Room supper was held in the Village Hall every year. A party of about 45 members and guests (presided over by the vicar, the Rev A.J. Wilcox) enjoyed a good meal and evening entertainment.

The Flower Show

WHEN THE FLOWER SHOW was revived after World War I it was held in the grounds of Bradley House and the adjoining park. It was usually held on the first Saturday in August and was always looked upon as the highlight of the year; nearly the whole village turned out for this event. It was organised by a committee headed by a chairman who was always the estate land agent. The secretary was the chief clerk in the Estate Office.

Several large marquees were hired to house all the exhibits and a number of smaller tents were provided by the estate as well. The staging and the poultry pens were also provided and erected by estate workers.

Herbert's Steam Fair and Amusements were always in attendance and would arrive from Dorchester the evening before the show. Most of the kids would go down Kingston Lane to see the performance of the massive steam engines manoeuvring the trailers loaded with the roundabouts, swinging boats and all the rest of the amusements through the gates at the Bull Shed into the park. It was quite a work of art to get the trailers through with only a few inches to spare. After a couple of years the show was held in Mr. Luff's field at the top of Kingston Lane where the amusements were able to enter much more easily.

According to records the first flower show was held in 1902 (when it was known as 'Maiden Bradley Horticultural Society') on the first Saturday in August. There is still a photograph in existence of this event. An old schedule shows that there was a total of 122 classes – vegetables, flowers, fruit, poultry, pigs, cottage gardens and allotments, as well as industrial classes, butter, jams, chutney and many more. The exhibits were divided into cottagers' classes

Maiden Bradley Flower Show and Sports 1912
Maiden Bradley Park
(Algernon Duke of Somerset wearing cap watching the Sports)

(parishoners only) and 'open' (to a radius of five miles). The open classes were patronised by exhibitors from Horningsham, Witham Friary, Kilmington and Stourton and district.

Money prizes were given for 1st, 2nd and 3rd in all classes. A number of special prizes were given by local seedsmen and corn merchants as well as medals and certificates from the gardening weeklies. There was usually a good entry in most classes as all the householders cultivated their gardens, while most had allotments as well. People would aim to grow enough vegetables to keep them supplied throughout the winter so, at Show time, they usually had a good choice of vegetables to pick from. The exhibits were always of a high quality and there was much rivalry amongst the exhibitors.

There were sports for adults and children and again prizes were awarded; these were mementoes and medals rather than money. There was dancing in one of the marquees with music provided by a brass band that had been playing at the show all afternoon. The beer tent was run by Wadworth's

Maiden Bradley Football Team 1921 (The Reserves)
Back Row left to right Vic Bailey (linesman), Wilf Cox, Basil Leather, unknown, Jack Seal
Second Row Joe Curtis, Bert Newbury, unknown.
Front Row Len Seaford, Edd Stone, Sam Biffen, George Snook, Harold White
Picture taken at Maiden Bradley Village Hall

brewery. The admission charge from 2-5 pm was a shilling and after 5 pm it was sixpence.

The Village Cricket and Football Teams

T HE CRICKET TEAM played their matches in a field belonging to Church Farm where a new pavilion was erected and fenced in. A good wicket area (with easily removable fencing) was made and a groundsman appointed to keep the pitch in good match play condition.

Maiden Bradley Football Team 1927
Maiden Bradley defeated Mere in the Warminster Hospital Cup that year.
Back Row Basil Leather, Fred Pearson, Edgar Howell, George Hill, Percy Timms, Len Seaford (Reserve)
Middle Row Sam Biffen, Jack Salvidge, Herb Salvidge, Albert Miles
Front Row Bob Phelps, Percy Walters (Captain), Bill Edwards

A committee of players' wives and friends was on hand to provide teas for players and officials at home matches. Quite a number of the local farmers played for the club. Mr. Bob Luff of Perry Farm was captain for many years; he was also known as a demon left arm slow bowler. The club kept going until 1939 when war was declared.

In the 1920s and onwards the village always had a football team and usually entered in the Warminster league as well as the Frome league, the Frome Hospital Cup and the Warminster Hospital Cup and usually did very well. In 1927 Maiden Bradley reached the final of the Warminster Hospital Cup which was played on the Warminster Town Football ground. The opponents were Mere (they had already won two cups that season) who were favourites to beat the underdogs Maiden Bradley. Nevertheless we won the cup which was presented by the Duke of Somerset, who commented how pleased he was to give it to our village team.

At that time Maiden Bradley did not have a recreation ground and it was left to the generosity of one of the local farmers to let people use a field for the season. Over the years a number of fields were used: Mr. Luff's field around Back Lane for a few seasons then Church Farm field for a number of years (next to the present recreation ground) and after that Mr. Ben Crees of Katesbench Farm provided a field up Hollow Lane.

Maiden Bradley Pig Club

AFTER A PIG CLUB was started in the village sties were erected by the estate on the members' gardens or allotments. This proved to be quite popular as there were between twenty and thirty members who each kept an average of three pigs in their sty.

At the flower show there were classes for the best pair of fat pigs, the best pair of store pigs (Large Whites) and the best pair of Large White Cross (not over five score). The prize money given for each class was seven and six for first, five shillings for second and three shillings for third – quite a substantial amount when you think that wages at the time were only thirty shillings per week. These classes were open to cottagers residing in Maiden Bradley, Gare Hill and Witham Friary.

The Duke of Somerset gave a cup at Frome Cheese Show for the best pair of porkers (not over eight score). This class attracted a number of entries from

Maiden Bradley and although open to all comers it was usually won by a member of our club.

The usual procedure for the people with pig sties was to buy in three or four little pigs from one of the local farmers and fatten them until they were nearly ten score in weight. They would keep one back for their own use and send the remaining ones to the bacon factory in Frome (Lewis's Pork Butchers).

As mentioned there was a licenced slaughterer in the village who would kill and cut up the pig you were keeping for your own use. It was a common sight to see hams and other parts of the pig hanging from hooks in the kitchens and outhouses of club members. The club flourished for a number of years.

The Estate Yard

THIS WAS A VERY BUSY PLACE where a lot of the village men were employed. The yard could be entered from Church Street or from the track leading from the Horsefair. There was a large shed that housed the sawmill, there was the carpenter's shop which was a sizeable place with four or five workbenches for carpenters and apprentices and also the painter's shop and store.

The stables and cart sheds were in the lower end of the yard where three heavy horses were kept for use on the Estate. Mr. Henry Doel was the carter who always had another man (or lad) to help him with the horses. Mr. Doel fetched timber from the estate woodlands back to the sawmills where it was sawn into board to be used for repairs to the houses and farms on the Estate. There was a large drying shed at the back of the sawmill where the board was stacked and seasoned before being used by the carpenters.

In the early 1920s the estate bought a Dennis 30 cwt lorry. They advertised in the local papers for a lorry driver and the successful applicant was Mr. Bill Humphries from Wincanton who remained in the job until his retirement. One of the open sheds at the bottom of the yard was made into a garage where the lorry could be locked in. It was estate policy to keep the lorry for three or four years and then trade it in for a new one (always a Dennis).

The lorry was kept busy hauling for the masons and carpenters or fetching coal for Bradley House. The house had coal fires as well as a coke-operated heating system – a lot of coal was used so they would have a ten ton truck of Midland coal (better than the coal from Radstock) delivered to Frome Station that Bill Humphries would collect.

There were usually three or four masons (each with a labourer) all kept busy with maintenance of properties in Maiden Bradley, Gare Hill and Witham Friary as well as on all the farms. Two painters were employed on the estate to

Estate carpenters, below: Jess Wilkins, Ray Newbury, Charlie Seal and Ted Dennis.

paint all the properties and by the time they had finished it was time for them to start all over again.

The carpenters, wearing their white aprons, could be seen in the village doing repairs and if the weather was not good enough to work outside they always had plenty of work to do in their workshop making windows and doors.

The plumber had quite a task keeping the waterworks in Maiden Bradley, Gare Hill and Witham Friary in working order but if there was a burst pipe underground the estate workers would be called in to do the digging. The plumber had a well equipped workshop stocked with the spare parts that would be needed in an emergency.

The Clerk of Works

THE ESTATE CLERK OF WORKS lived in the house at the entrance to the Estate Yard (now Home Farmhouse). He was in charge of the workmen and of all the goings on in the yard. Before the men came to work in the morning a list would be posted up in the porch of his house where they could see their orders for the day if they had not had them previously. The working day started at 6.30 am, there was a break for breakfast from 8–8.30 am and dinner (never called lunch) time was from 1–2 pm with the day ending at 5 pm. On Saturdays they worked from 6.30 am until 12.30 pm.

By 8 am in the morning William Viney, the engine driver, had steam up and would blow a hooter to let the men know it was breakfast time. He would also give another blast to let them know it was time to come back to work. He sounded the hooter at 1 pm, 2 pm and at 5 pm to signal the end of the day. This procedure continued for a number of years until the steam engine was replaced with a big powerful diesel engine.

The Saw Mill

THE MACHINERY in the mill consisted of rack-benches, planers, more small saws and a band saw. They were all powered by the big steam engine which needed a full-time engine driver (William Viney) as mentioned above. The head sawyer, Mr. John Mounty, was very precise in everything he did; he kept a record of all the sawn timber in the drying shed and made sure no timber was taken out unless properly seasoned.

There was always a good supply of round timber (ash, oak, beech, elm, pine and larch) stacked behind the mill ready for John Mounty and his team to get to work on. All the timber had been grown on the estate, cut by the forestry workers and fetched from the woods by the estate horses and timber carriages.

The Duke of Somerset's Estate Land Agent

THE AGENT lived in the 'Cottage' (as it was called years ago) which is now called the Old Dower House. A gardener/handyman was employed full-time to keep the gardens and lawns in good condition and he usually produced enough vegetables to keep the household supplied throughout the year. The gardener lived nearby in 12 Church Street. The agent and his wife, Mr. and Mrs. Russell Taylor, with their two children Jeffrey and Mary employed six servants in the house – a nanny, a cook and two housemaids (all living in) as well as two women to run the adjoining laundry.

Bradley House

THE DUKE AND DUCHESS OF SOMERSET lived at Bradley House and employed a large staff of servants. The butler was in charge of the footman and hall boy. The butler, Mr. Seaford, lived next to the nurse in High Street, while the footman, Fred Pearson, and Clarence Blacker, the hall boy, both lived in Bradley House.

Miss Mary Gray, who was the elderly housekeeper, was very strict with the staff of girls that were needed to run the house. There were usually as many as ten servants comprising a 'sewing person' in charge of household repairs, housemaids (head and under), kitchen maids, parlour maids, scullery maids and cooks (head and under). A handyman was employed to supply wood and coal ready to keep all the fires going in the House.

Maiden Bradley Ex-Service Men
After inspection by H.R.H. Prince of Wales, Bradley House 1923
Among the men on parade are:- Major W.L. Barton and R. Gifford M.C.
H. Flower, H. Viney, H. White, B.C. Leather, G. Flower, G. Dredge, A. Flower,
L. Newbury, J. Seal, J. Spurle, A. Dredge, S. Blackband, G. Dulake, A. Doman,
E. Newbury, P, Newbury, C. Merritt, A. Seaford, H. Smith, A. Reed, A. Payne

Bradley House staff, picknicking on the lawn, 1919

A chauffeur, Mr. Read, was on hand with the Daimler limousine which was always kept well polished and was used mostly by the Duchess. Horses were more favoured by the Duke who could often be seen riding around the village and the surrounding woods.

Two local women worked doing the laundry for the Duke and Duchess and the staff – very much a full-time job!

The Stables

THE STABLES were always busy. A number of hunters were kept as well as carriage horses. The head coachman was Mr. Aldridge who lived in the Lodge. There was also an under coachman, Mr. J. Seal (Senior), who lived at Kingston Lane Cottages as well as two grooms (Jack Seal Junior and Harry Biffen). The grooms could be seen early in the mornings exercising the horses, usually riding one and leading one, and they would often do 4–6 miles before breakfast. The stables were kept spotlessly clean as they were liable to be inspected by the Duke and Duchess at any time.

The grooms were responsible for keeping the harness room and all the harness well polished. The sets of harness kept on 'wooden horses' were those that were only used on state occasions. In the early 1920s whenever the Duke and Duchess attended the Opening of Parliament the State carriage and horses would be taken to Frome Station and put on the train to London. They would be taken off the train at Paddington and driven to Grosvenor Square where the Duke had a town house and

Jack Seal (groom to the Duke of Somerset) and one of the Bradley House servants have just cleaned the State Coach ready for use.
Picture taken from outside the coach house in the Stable Yard.

where the horses would stay at a mews nearby. A head coachman, footman and groom would be in charge of the arrangements; the horses were allowed to be exercised in Hyde Park before 7 am any morning.

On the day when Parliament was to be opened the state carriage would collect the Duke and Duchess, wearing all their regalia, from the house in Grosvenor Square and the head coachman (accompanied by the footman, both in their 'flunky' gear) would drive to the Palace of Westminster. I have been told (by Jack Seal, my brother-in-law) what a wonderful sight it was to see all the carriages arrive with their occupants in their beautiful ceremonial robes. The carriage would be cleaned on returning to Maiden Bradley and put away ready for the next time. The harness would be cleaned and returned to the 'wooden horse' where all the leather straps would be treated with neatsfoot oil and all the nickel parts wrapped in tissue paper so that it would be ready for the next occasion.

A special horse was kept for station wagon duties because goods for use at Bradley House would come into Frome Station and be fetched by Mr. Seal (Senior). The horse was a good trotter and made light work of the journey to Frome, sometimes two or three times a week.

As previously mentioned a two-wheeled trap was available if the village nurse was called to outlying parts of the estate.

Bradley House Gardens

THE GARDENS (including the frame yard and lower garden) were tended by a team of six or more gardeners. The greenhouses were kept well stocked as the house, with its huge staff, needed a large supply of fruit and vegetables for the whole year. The lawns were cut by Jack Seal using a horse-drawn mower although in later years Dennis motor mowers were purchased to do this job more quickly.

Home Farm

THE HOME FARM with its herd of Guernsey cows was managed by the estate (who employed a cowman) to keep the house supplied with milk, butter and eggs throughout the year. Other work on the farm was done by the estate workers with the mowing, haymaking and harvest done by Mr. Doel and the estate horses.

Algernon, 15th Duke of Somerset, and Susan, Duchess of Somerset

THEY LIVED IN BRADLEY HOUSE and had no offspring, and they let it be known that when they died they wished to be buried in Brimble Hill Clump (a clump of trees on rising ground in Bradley Park about half a mile from Bradley House). Algernon died first and after the funeral service in Bradley Church the coffin was taken on one of the Duke's wagons across the fields to the Clump for the burial service. Four horses were used to pull the wagon, two of the Duke's black horses and two grey horses that had been loaned for the occasion by Sir Henry Hoare of Stourhead.

The wagon and horses had been well turned out for the occasion. The wagon had been painted slate grey and the horses and all the harness looked immaculate as did the two bowler-hatted grooms in charge of the horses. It was said to be a sight of a lifetime. The funeral was attended by lords and ladies from all over the country; many mourners came by train to Frome and a bus was laid on, as well as taxis, to bring them out to the village.

Employment

IN THE EARLY 1920s most of the village houses were occupied by people who worked on the estate or on the estate farms. The farms had not yet become mechanised and so the ploughing was all done by horses and the cows were milked by hand. To cope with all the work the farmers had to employ a lot of labour so when the boys left school (at the age of fourteen) there was usually a job awaiting them either on the estate or on the farms.

The Estate Forestry Department

A NUMBER OF MEN were employed to keep the woods tidy and productive – a Bradley gang and a Gare Hill gang, with up to eight men in each of them. There was always plenty of work to do – timber to be cut, plantations to be kept trimmed as well as roads and paths to be kept in good order. From time to time new plantations were planted on areas that had been clear felled. With the amount of labour available the woods were kept in first class condition.

In wet weather when the men were unable to work outside in the open they would go to the 'pickling tank' where there was a job under cover. The pickling tank consisted of three or four large sheds where stakes were made and stacked; they were then passed on to a unit where the stakes were pickled in boiling creosote. There was a great demand for stakes as many were used in the woods to fence in the new plantations against rabbits and for maintenance of the farm fences.

The estate sold a great number of trees to timber merchants in the area and these were removed from the woods using big steam engines, so the estate roads needed quite a lot of repair. The estate also sold 'parcels' (as they were known) or plots of underwood to local wood merchants. This underwood was worked up into a variety of products. Pea and bean sticks and faggots were made out of the brushwood; poles of ash and alder would go for rails and stakes while some of the bigger timber would go for pit props or firewood. Everything was useful – nothing was wasted. The wood merchants had quite a good sale for all these items and there was always a demand for firewood as everyone in the village relied on wood and coal for heating and cooking.

Frank White (holding the crosscut saw), Foreman of the Bradley Estate woodmen with his gang equipped for timber felling. On the left with axe and billhook is Mathew Henry Sims (grandfather of the Author), who died in 1934 aged 99, thus dating the photograph around 1890. The sledgehammer and felling wedge were used to topple the tree without pinching the saw.

The Local Farmers

I T WAS A SLOWER LIFE in Maiden Bradley in the 1920s, much more relaxed and still very much relying on horse transport. On a Wednesday quite a few farmers from Kilmington, Stourton, Mere, Zeals and Bourton would pass through the village on their way to Frome Market with their ponies and traps and most of them would stop at the fountain to let the pony have a well earned drink of water.

On Frome Cheese Show day farmers passed through the village on route to the show. On the return journey they would stop at the fountain for the pony to have a drink and the next stop was at Bradley pub where the farmer would also have a drink. We kids would wait outside the pub and offer to hold the pony while they were having their refreshments, and after having a good day at the show some of them were in a generous mood and we would go home with a pocket full of coppers.

All the farmers in the village in the early twenties had a motor car, with the exception of Mr. Lester of Manor Farm, Yarnfield who would travel to Market in his pony and trap. However in 1923 when Basil Leather started running his bus to Frome on Wednesdays Mr. Lester would walk to Bradley and go to Frome on the bus. If he was too heavily laden with shopping he would hire the taxi to take him back to Yarnfield. Although he farmed Manor Farm until he retired in the mid-1930s he never had a car and always travelled by either horse transport or taxi.

There were no cattle lorries in the early twenties and when the farmers had cattle to go to market drovers were hired to drive them (on foot) to either Warminster or Frome. The farmer selling the cattle would go by car to see the animals sold, then collect the money and bring the drovers back to Bradley. Two local men, Arthur Newbury and Arthur Dredge, worked at Church Farm and acted as drovers for Mr. Jeffries for many years. They continued this job until cattle trucks became popular.

Most of the local farmers would fetch their cattle feeds by horse and wagon from Frome station where it would come by the truck load. As years progressed all the cattle feed was delivered to the farms by the corn and feed merchants from around the district.

Haymaking and Harvest

B EFORE THE DAYS of the tractor in the early 1920s the farmers relied on horses and a lot of casual labour to get in the hay and the harvest. It was mostly hay that was made then, very few farmers made silage. Some of the bigger lads of the village would spend their weekends and school holidays working on the farms to earn a few shillings, some of them adapted themselves to farm work and made it a career on leaving school at the age of fourteen. Estate workers would also help the farmers out in the busy season – they were glad of the overtime pay and it suited the farmer to have extra labour.

The mowing was done by two horses pulling a mowing machine and on some of the larger farms there were often two teams of horses working in the same field. They usually made an early start at around 4 am as they used to say that the grass was easier to cut in the early morning before the sun came up.

The farmers would send their haymaking machinery to the local blacksmiths to be checked over before the season started to make sure that they were in good working order. They consisted of a mowing machine, swath turner, tedding machine, side rake and horse rake. A supply of spare knives for the mower was always needed, with constant sharpening they soon wore out.

When the hay was ready to be picked up the side rake would come into action and roll the hay into long rolls across the field. Large farm wagons with their hay racks attached would then be loaded; one man at each side of the wagon pitched the hay on and another man on the wagon loaded it. The load would then be taken into the farm rickyard and unloaded on to the rick. When haymaking was completed the ricks would be thatched to keep the hay dry until it was needed in the cowstall for winter feed. It was a very pleasing sight for the farmer to see all the ricks lined up in the rickyard, thatched and looking so tidy.

There was an old custom that lasted many years – in the spring the farmers would all get in a good stock of farmhouse cider in readiness for the workers during haymaking and harvest time. Jars of this cider and cider-mugs were kept at some convenient spot in the field where the men could stop work and have a well earned drink when necessary. When the jars became empty during the evening one of the boys would take them back to the farm to be refilled!

When the corn was ready to be cut the binder was brought into action. The binder was a machine drawn by two horses that would cut the corn and tie it into sheaves which were dropped behind the machine as it covered the field. They were later stacked into 'hiles' to dry before being gathered up and hauled in on wagons to be put into ricks. These were then thatched to keep the sheaves dry until later on in the winter when the threshing machine would come to finish the operation.

There was one threshing machine in the village which was owned by the Jeffries family of Church Farm. As well as doing all their own, they would do threshing for the other farmers in the village. It was quite a performance getting the threshing machinery set up and it was an exciting time for the children to go around the farms and watch the threshing being undertaken. It needed three horses to pull the big portable steam engine and sometimes four horses to pull the threshing machine from Church Farm. An engine driver (Fred Elliott) would be in attendance the whole time the engine was working and he had to make sure he had plenty of coal and water to keep it going. It needed another three or four workers for various jobs on the thresher. The sheaves were pitched from the rick to the top of the thresher where Mrs. Bessie Ball would cut the bonds and pass the sheaf on to George Dredge who would feed it into the machine. More men were at the back of the thresher to bag up the corn and take away the straw and caving, also kids would come armed with sticks hoping to knock over any rats or mice that may pop out of the rick where they had been living during the winter.

Village Life

THE AMOUNT OF TRAFFIC passing through the village in the early twenties was negligible. It was so little that girls could enjoy an uninterrupted game of hop-scotch or skipping and the boys played marbles or ball games in the street. It was a common sight to see the hop scotch pitches and the marble rings marked out on the road in white chalk all down through the street. I have seen the girls remain standing on the hop-scotch pitch and make the passing lorry drive around them when they were in the middle of a game!

There was no radio (or wireless as it was called in those days) with the exception of the Post Office which had an old set. If there was a good programme on a summer's evening they would open the window and face the loud speaker towards the road so that villagers could stand outside and listen. My auntie (Mrs. Charles Newbury) had a crystal set and when I fetched her milk at 5 pm each evening from Mr. Doman's she would, as a treat, let me hear the wireless. She would fix me up with a pair of headphones and fiddle with the cats whisker on the crystal until she got reception- quite a hit or miss business. Later on wireless sets became more popular and to get a good reception it was necessary to have an outdoor aerial strung from two poles in the garden, usually fifteen or twenty feet high and twenty to thirty yards apart.

A few people in the village had gramophones to provide the family entertainment during the winter's evenings. Some of the older men were regulars in the local pub for their nightly drink and a chat, while the younger lads would go to the Reading Room for a game of billiards or cards.

During the winter time a travelling concert party would come to the village and book the hall for three weeks and perform concerts and variety shows. They usually got a good response from the local people as well as from the surrounding villages – there were often as many as sixty people present. The party that came to Maiden Bradley was called 'Freddy Fay's Frolics' and they performed their summer season at Burnham-on-Sea. They would lodge in the village during the period they performed here and they continued to come for a number of years, becoming well-known throughout the district.

During the spring and summer evenings the men were busy on their gardens and most had allotments as well. The idea was to grow enough vegetables to keep the household supplied throughout the year.

Maiden Bradley Football Team 1923
Back Row (left to right): Basil Leather, Sid Harris, Les Marshall, Ray Newbury, Jim Dickinson, Harry White, Lewis Newbury (Linesman)
Second Row: Bert Newbury, Edgar Howell, Bob Phelps, Sam Biffen, Jess Trollope
Front Row: Ern Smith, Bill Snook.

A number of villagers were keen supporters of the football and cricket teams and would spend Saturday afternoons cheering on their side at all the home matches. No sport was ever played on Sundays, but people went to Church or Chapel and enjoyed a Sunday afternoon walk. A favourite walk for a lot of families was through Penny's and Bradley woods, particularly in the spring when the long avenues of azaleas and rhododendrons were in bloom. The lovely aroma of the flowers was always appreciated and it was quite often possible to meet forty people from the village when walking in the woods. Another walk that was enjoyed by the more energetic folk was to go to the top of Bradley Knoll where, on a nice day, it was possible to enjoy the view over many miles around.

Although the Football Club and the Cricket Club each had their fields where they played their matches there was no recreation field for the children. However George Locke never seemed to mind when the children played in his field at the back of the houses in Church Street.

The boys, particularly the older ones, would go bird nesting in the spring and summer and most boys had collections of eggs – the rule was to take only one egg from each nest. The Headmaster had a large collection of eggs that were all mounted and named. They were kept in glass cases in large cupboards with glass doors at the school. Some of the contents of these cupboards – eggs, snakes, wasp and bees' nests, fossils etc. found their way into Devizes and Exeter museums when Mr. Scanes retired.

Most of the farms in and around the village had ponds (many long since gone) where moorhens and wild ducks nested. Taking a few eggs for the collections did not appear to affect the bird population. It was only many years later when hundreds of miles of hedgerows were grubbed out all over the country and new farming techniques started that the bird population began to diminish.

The estate gamekeepers would restrict access to certain roads and paths in the woods in the spring when the pheasant rearing season was in progress. Hundreds of pheasants were reared each year; eggs were bought in and hatched under broody hens in one of the farmer's fields. When they were a few weeks old they would be transferred to pens in the woods and kept under supervision by the keepers. One keeper would be on duty all night to make sure none were taken away by foxes. They would have a shepherd's hut on site where they were able to brew up a cup of tea and just relax for a while. Pheasant rearing was big business in the 1920s.

During the winter months the Head Keeper (Mr. G. Dulake) would organise deer shooting parties on the Bradley Estate. The shooters usually

Deer-shooting party

consisted of keepers from neighbouring estates as well as local farmers and a few businessmen from Frome. These shoots were necessary to keep the deer population down. The deer that were killed were butchered and the venison joints were handed out to the shooters and beaters.

Rook-shooting parties were held at the rookery (Park Knoll) on three or four evenings each year before nesting time to keep the population at bay. This annual event attracted a few businessmen from Frome as well as a few local farmers and friends. The keepers would encourage the local lads to come along and pick up the birds when they had been shot. The rooks were then tied up into bundles of six and were given to anyone who would like to take them home to make a pie.

In the early 1920s, before wireless sets were popular, it was difficult to get accurate time checks to set your watch. I remember asking my grandfather 'What's the time Gramph?' He carefully took his solid silver pocket watch out of his waistcoat pocket, looked at it for a couple of seconds and then said 'Well I can only tell 'ee Frome time and that was set by the Wallbridge hooter (Frome) at 8 o'clock this morning'. It all depended, of course, on the direction the wind was blowing, sometimes the Warminster or even the Bourton foundry hooter could be heard more plainly. Sometimes Warminster and Frome time varied as much as four minutes.

When it came to forecasting the weather some of the old men of the village could give a pretty accurate account of what weather we would be getting for the next few days. They studied the winds, clouds, the moon and lots of other things and could usually be relied upon to be 75% right. We appeared to have more severe winter weather in those days with plenty of snow, but better summers with lots of sunshine and warm weather. When heavy snow blocked the roads Bradley was cut off for sometimes three or four days at a time. As there was no mechanical means of clearing the snow everything had to be done by manual labour, and gangs of men were recruited to dig a track wide enough to allow vehicles through.

The Wiltshire County Council (Roads Department) kept a horse-drawn snow plough in the village for use around the area. The Council had an agreement with the local contractor Mr. Doman (later Mr. Leather) allowing him to send his horses out with the plough on snowy days when he thought it necessary, sometimes it needed as many as six horses to pull the plough. The plough only worked when the snow was no more than about two feet deep; if deeper it needed the shovel gangs in action.

Snow digging at Baycliffe, Christmas 1927
Fred Flower, Arthur Ball, Sam Biffen, Charlie Sims, Joe Curtis,
Don Newbury, Frank Doman, Bert Butcher and Harry Doel.
Picture taken by Basil Leather

The agricultural as well as estate and forestry workers' wages in the twenties were one pound ten shillings a week – it was known as ''30 bob a week'. With one shilling and threepence deducted for National Insurance the take home pay was one pound eight shillings and nine pence. There was no children's allowance or any other state benefit. It must have been hard times for some of the parents who had families to feed and clothe on the meagre wages, and there was but very little scope for luxuries after all the weekly bills were paid.

People did not go to Frome shopping very often; most things could be bought in the village either from our local shop, Walton's, or from tradesmen who came to the village selling their wares. Leathers of Kilmington and Co-op of Mere each had a regular bread round in the village. Three butchers, Co-op of Mere, Chinns of Warminster and Hayward & Taylor of Frome, also had rounds in the village. Fred Witcombe, a fishmonger from Frome, came to Maiden Bradley with fresh fish at 7.30 am on Wednesdays and Saturdays. The fish had travelled from Grimsby by train through the night and arrived at Frome Station at 5.30 am where it was picked up by 'Fishy Whitcombe' and by 8 am he had supplied quite a number of customers in Maiden Bradley – a very welcome service.

Penroses of Frome also came to the village on a weekly basis. They sold ladies' clothes and household goods – everything that was needed in the home. Men's clothing was supplied by John Dance who had shops in Frome as well as a weekly round in the village. Haskells of Frome came to Bradley on Tuesdays to sell footwear, and took boots and shoes to be repaired, which they brought back on a Thursday.

People could just stay in their homes and get everything they needed brought to them without having the expense of going to Frome. The tradesmen that came to the village selling their wares would let their clients pay a few shillings a week, as very few people had enough money to pay for the article outright. These traders were known as 'Johnny Fortnight' traders.

During the period from the end of World War I in 1918 to the end of World War II in 1945 only two houses were built in the parish. These were two built by the estate at Newmead for farm workers in 1920/21 (the two red brick houses at the top of the track leading to the Farm). The houses were built by Messrs. Culverhouse of Chapmanslade and were a good asset as farm workers were in great demand in those days. Some of the workers who came to Newmead had very large families – up to eight children sometimes – but would stay just a few weeks and be gone again, unable to see eye to eye with Mr. Beak.

There were seven farm cottages at Rodmead, although some years later when there was not as much demand for farm workers three of the cottages were pulled down. Several other houses that stood a little way out of the village have also now been taken down; two at Yarnfield (Bileshole Bottom and Yarnfield Bottom, the latter having had a thatched roof caught fire and burned down) together with a rank of three cottages at Dunkerton (numbers 96, 97 and 98) and two cottages by the side of the Mill Pond (numbers 101 and 102). Bricefield Cottage (number 5 and in the early days occupied by one of the Duke's keepers) was still in use until after World War II when it was partly demolished. The keeper's cottage at Gare Hill (now part of 'Tyning Wood') also burned down as a result of a chimney and thatched roof fire.

There was no refuse collection and as all the houses had open fireplaces or ranges there were plenty of ashes to be disposed of. All refuse had to be taken to the quarry and dumped – it was a common sight to see the men struggling up there in the evenings and at weekends with sacks of rubbish on their backs. The quarry was up the lane to the left just past the recreation field.

In the early 1920s there were limited means available to villagers wishing to communicate with anyone living outside the village but there was a very reliable postal service. A letter posted before 8 pm at Bradley Post Office was usually any-where in the country the following day. There was no first and second class postage – just the one, each stamp costing 'three ha'pence'. There was no public telephone until one was installed in the Blind House (the old village lock-up adjoining the Post Office) and then this service was only available during opening hours.

When Basil Leather took over the carrier's and coal and wood business in 1923 and had the telephone installed he was allocated the number Maiden Bradley 13. This meant that there were only thirteen subscribers on the Maiden Bradley exchange which included Horningsham, Longleat and others.

When villagers were taken ill and needed a doctor the usual procedure was to get someone to cycle over to Bourton to the doctor's surgery with a message. The doctor would respond pretty quickly, usually getting over to Bradley before the cyclist had returned!

If you needed to send an urgent message this could be done by sending a telegram. You would go to the Post Office and ask for a telegram form on which you wrote the message. You always kept the message very brief as you were charged according to the number of words on the form. If a telegram arrived at Bradley Post Office for someone in the village the postmaster would either deliver it or get one of his children to bring it. They would always wait to see if there was a reply.

Maiden Bradley Post Office worked in conjunction with Horningsham on early closing days. If a telegram was sent to someone in Bradley on early closing day (Wednesday afternoon) this would automatically come to Horningsham and either their postmaster would walk up to Bradley and deliver it or else get someone with a bike to bring it up. The same arrangements applied when Horningsham was closed on Thursdays and the Bradley postmaster was responsible for delivering the telegrams to Horningsham.

There were of course no automatic telephone exchanges in those days. On picking up the phone the local operator would ask 'Number please' and it could be quite a long wait getting connected through the exchanges if it happened to be a long distance call.

On Empire Day each year it was the custom for the Duke and Duchess to come to school where the Union Flag was hoisted on the flagpole. All the children and teachers gathered around and patriotic songs were sung with the Duke and Duchess joining in. It appears that this ceremony had been carried out for many years, as can be seen from a photograph taken in 1908.

Maiden Bradley Empire Day Celebrations 1908
The Duke and Duchess always attended the ceremony

The Service of Remembrance was always held on 11th November in the evening but if the 11th fell on a Sunday then the service would be held in the morning. The ex-servicemen (British Legion members) would line up in High Street outside the Village Hall and march down to the Church headed by Zeals

Silver Band, who would go in to the Church and play the hymns, and one of the bandsmen would sound the Last Post. The Church was always crowded on this occasion. After the service the parade would line up outside the Church and march back to the Village Hall where refreshments were served. The parade attracted as many as forty ex-servicemen, quite often coming from Kilmington and Horningsham to join the march. The service was a solemn occasion as many who attended had lost relatives in the recent war.

Maiden Bradley ex-service men and scouts being inspected by H.R.H. Prince of Wales.
Bradley House 1923.
The school children were also present at the ceremony
Standing in the front is R. Gifford (of Rodmead Farm) who was awarded the Military Cross.
With the Prince of Wales is Major W.L. Barton (the Duke's agent) and Algernon Duke of
Somerset following behind (the tall man with the trilby hat).

Most of the cottages in the village, in addition to having gardens adjoining their houses, had allotments as well. Some of the allotments were on the Bruton road on land between Quarry Lane and the main road, others were on the Frome road just past Laurel Farm, and the rest were in High Street between the Village Hall and the Police Station with more beyond it. All the latter have now been built on.

Since the 1920s some of the old village names have faded out. If you came up through Church Street and turned left at the crossroads you would then be going up 'Horsefair' and the junction at the top of Horsefair by Quarry Lane and the entrance to the allotments was known as 'the Pound'. I expect one would need to delve more deeply into the village history to find out where these two names came from. The crossroads was a favourite meeting place for village lads who seemed to congregate by the Knapp railings for hours exchanging yarns. If you wanted to meet someone you would usually say 'I will meet you up on the corner' and it was always known as the corner never the crossroads.

At the bottom end of the village between Church Farm fields and the Vicarage there is a ditch that takes away the water from Boreham and after heavy rain this gets full up and overflows into the road. The water goes through a tunnel under the road that was known as 'Minny Tunnel' and which we kids would explore with a candle when the weather was favourable. The road from Minny Tunnel up to the Rodmead turning was known as 'Whitepell'. The field that runs from the Rodmead turning towards Mere was not fenced on the Rodmead Road side and was known as 'Three Acres'. It was supposedly common land so travellers and gypsies often camped there and grazed their horses.

There was a village custom that lasted many years and only came to an end when World War II started in 1939. The lads of the village would go each year on Palm Sunday afternoon up on the roadside of Long Knoll armed with hockey sticks (or walking sticks) and play hockey. The idea was to knock the ball to the top of the hill – a difficult job as the hill was very steep and the ball would roll back down again. This was the only day of the year the sport was allowed.

Another meeting place for the lads was at the 'Horse Pond' which was at Perry Farm opposite the junction to Back Lane. It was a good clean pond free of weed and regularly used by Mr. Luff's ducks. When the weather was frosty and the pond frozen over it was a good place for skating. It was fenced off on the roadside with strong railings, painted white and about 2ft 6 in high, just the right height to sit on and take a quiet rest – which was what the locals often did.

The long dark winter evenings were very dreary for the local school children with no wireless or television and the majority of families did not have a gramophone. If you had brothers and sisters you stayed in and played cards or board games such as snakes and ladders to pass away the evening. I was one on my own so I usually went out and met up with some of the other boys and just walked around the streets or sat on the Knapp railings and had a yarn – sometimes we played games. We quite often went over to a friend's home where we were invited to stay to supper – bread and cheese and a cup of cocoa. We had to keep a wary eye open for the policeman because if he caught us running around the streets or even sitting on the railings we were liable for a hefty clout with his rolled cape.

The Duchess laid on a lavish Christmas party for the children of the village as well as those from Gare Hill and Witham Friary. It was held in the Village Hall with presents for everyone and with a bus hired to fetch the children from outside. Susan Duchess always seemed to be interested in the welfare of the village people and liked to be kept informed if anyone was ill and needed help. She was known to send up hot meals from Bradley House kitchens and generally keep an eye on them until they were better.

On summer evenings we usually stayed outside till it got dark enjoying a game of cricket or football. We made our own cricket bats and wickets and for football we would go down to the shop to get a pig's bladder which we would blow up and kick around.

Maiden Bradley Scouts 1912. The Duke of Somerset's Own Troop, formed in 1910.
Photograph taken in camp at Newclose

Scouts

THE DUKE OF SOMERSET'S OWN TROOP was formed in 1910. The Scoutmaster was the agent and the Deputy was Mr. J. Wilkins who later took over as Scoutmaster with Charles Seal as Deputy. They regularly camped in New Close where they could enjoy swimming in the scout pond. In later years they camped at Shearwater.

Maiden Bradley School Outing to Bristol Zoo 1921
The older children were allowed to ride in the charabanc and younger children rode in the bus.
Note the solid tyres on both vehicles, also the picking up point in the middle of the crossroads.
Mr. Scanes took this photograph from over in the school garden.

Personal Thoughts

I WELL REMEMBER the early 1920s as they were my school days. I started school in 1918 and by 1921 I was moving from the infants room where I had been taught by Miss Nellie Gillanders (later she was to become Mrs. Leather and later on again my boss) to the middle room where my teacher would be Mrs. Ludlow.

I can also remember 1921 as this was the only year during my school days that we had a school outing. Mr. Scanes organised an outing to Bristol Zoo on which most of the children went. He hired a bus and a charabanc – the small children rode in the bus and the older ones were allowed to ride in the charabanc. I think Mr. Scanes was just as excited about the trip as the children. In spite of the vehicle having solid tyres and pretty hard seats we still had a wonderful day out. Most of the children had never been to a zoo before so it was an outing that was remembered for many years.

People often talk of the 'Good Old Days' but the reality of living in the 1920s was that times were hard for a lot of the village families. The cost of living was cheap but even so, for many of the families with three or four children, it was a meagre existence feeding and clothing everyone on thirty shillings a week.

There is a saying 'What you haven't got you don't miss' – well we had no electricity in those days, we relied on candles and oil lamps. I wonder sometimes how we managed in the winter having to come downstairs with only the light of a candle. Then to get the first cup of tea the fire had to be lit to boil the kettle (after going outside the back door to fetch water) and it was usually half an hour before you could enjoy that first cup.

I think the greatest disadvantage of living in the village in those days (and even the '30s and '40s) was the primitive toilet arrangements. All the households had bucket toilets built by the estate carpenters (some had brick or stone built ones) in the back gardens as far as forty yards from the back door. They were known as sentry boxes. Also you may be able to imagine what a performance it was on bath nights (especially for large families) when you had a bath in front of the fire in a long galvanised tin tub before going to bed.

This was the way of life people were used to and it was accepted as normal. In spite of all the drawbacks people were happy to live in Maiden Bradley where there was always a friendly atmosphere – someone would always come to your assistance should you need help.

People Living in Maiden Bradley after the Great War

Kingston Lane

Newmead Farm	J.D. Beak	Farmer
	H. Beak (Son)	Farmer
Cottages No. 1 & No. 2		Occupied by Farm Workers
Kingston Lane Cottages		
No.1	John Seal	Under Coachman to Duke of Somerset
	J. Seal (Junior)	Groom (Bradley House)
	C. Seal	Carpenter (Estate)
No.1a	J. Dilworth	Butler (Bradley House)
No.2	L. Read	Chauffeur (Bradley House)

Back Lane

The Lodge	H. Aldridge	Head Coachman to Duke of Somerset
No.3	R. Prowse	Gardener (Bradley House Gardens)
No.4	J. Booton	Cowman (Duke of Somerset's Home Farm)
Rodmead Farm	A.J. Gifford & Sons	Farmers
Cottages	H. Payne and other farm Workers	
Bricefield Cottage (No.5)	W. Jones	Keeper (Estate)

Church Street

The Vicarage	A.J. Wilcox	Vicar
Church Farm	A. Jefferies	Farmer & Magistrate
	H. Jefferies (Son)	Farmer
	C. Jefferies (Son)	Farmer
No.6/7 Sunnyside	Capt. Hamilton-Bates	Retired Royal Navy
No.8	J. Rigby	Head Gardener (Bradley House)
No.9	Lue Beale	Laundry Worker (The Cottage)
The Cottage	R. Taylor	Land Agent to the Duke of Somerset
No. 10	C. Bealing	Blacksmith (for A.J. Baker)
No. 11	L. White	Farm Worker (Newmead Farm)

No. 12	B. Toogood	Gardener (The Cottage)
Estate Yard	W. Adams	Clerk of Works (Estate)
Orchard House	Mr. T. Carder	Retired Estate Manager
No. 13	C. Ford	Labourer (Estate)
No. 14	A. White	Head Carter (Church Farm)
No. 15	Mrs. Biffen	Laundry Worker (The Cottage)
	H. Biffen	Groom (Bradley House)
No. 16	G. Flower	Mason (Estate)
No. 17	G. Edwards	Estate Worker (Handyman)
No. 18	G. Adlam	Carpenter (Estate)
Walton's Stores	J. Gibbons	General Manager
	Miss K. Gibbons	Office Clerk
	Miss L. Gibbons	Drapery Manager
Somerset Arms	A.G. Locke	Landlord & Farmer
	Miss N. Locke (Sister)	Seen to every day workings of Pub
No. 19	W. Newbury	Farm Worker (Rodmead Farm)
No. 20	J. Wilkins	Carpenter (Estate)
No. 21	H. Flower	Labourer (Estate)
No. 22/23	H. Doel	Carter (Estate)
No. 24	H. Snook	Farm Worker (Rodmead Farm)
No. 25	H. Forcyth	Estate Worker
No. 26	W. Viney	Engine Driver (Estate Sawmill)
No. 27	G. Pole	Farm Manager (Dangell's Farm for G. Locke)
No. 28	Mrs. Pole	Widow
No. 29	R. Mounty	Boot & Shoe Repairer (worked from 29)
No. 30	Mrs. Bailey	Widow
	V. Bailey	Farm Worker (Katesbench Farm)
No. 31	W. Mounty (Shep)	Retired Shepherd (?)
No. 32	Mrs. (Granny) Ford	Widow
No. 33	G. Dredge	Farm Worker (Church Farm)
No. 34	R. Miles	Farmer, Egg & Butter Wholesaler
No. 35	G. Waters	Mason (Bradley Estate & Chimney Sweep)
No. 36	G. Curtis	Mason (Estate)
	J. Curtis	Mason (Estate)
No. 37	Mrs. T. Miles	Widow (Laundry Worker, The Cottage)
	J. Miles (Son)	Farm Worker (Rodmead Farm)
No. 38	F. Howell	Retired Plumber (Estate)
	Mrs. Smart (Daughter)	Widow
	L. Smart (Son)	Carpenter (Estate)
No. 39	G. Howell	Postman
	E. Howell	Farm Worker (Church Farm)
No. 40	H. May	Carpenter (A.J. Baker)

No. 41	J. May (Son)	Farm Worker (Baycliffe Farm)
No. 42	A. Griffen	Post Master & Blacksmith (A.J. Baker)
	A. Griffen (Son)	Village Garage Proprietor
	M. Griffen (Son)	Helping with the Garage
	I. Griffen (Daughter)	Working in the Post Office
	M. Griffen (Daughter)	Working in Telephone Exchange
	I. Griffen (Son)	General helper in the business
No. 43	J. Elsworth	Baker (for Walton's Stores)
	G. Elsworth (Son)	Farm Worker (Church Farm)
No. 44	J. Mounty	Head Sawyer (Estate)
No. 45	H. Dredge	Farm Worker (Perry Farm)
	J. Dredge (Son)	Forestry Worker
	A. Dredge (Son)	Farm Worker (Perry Farm)
No. 46	J. Newbury	Farm Worker (Church Farm)
	A. Newbury (Son)	Farm Worker (Church Farm)
No. 47	W. Nutley	Farm Worker (Newmead Farm)
No. 48	A.J. Baker	Owner of Blacksmiths & Wheelrights etc
	L. Baker (Son)	Carpenter for Bakers etc.
No. 49	F. Newbury (My Father)	Forestry Worker (Estate)
	F. Newbury (Daughter)	Housemaid (The Cottage)
	M. Sims (My Grandfather)	Retired – odd job man at Bradley House
No. 50 The Knapp	C. Newbury	Postman (Bradley Post Office)
	L. Newbury (Son)	Motor Engineer (Warminster Motor Co.)
	M. Newbury (Son)	Forestry Worker (Estate)
	R. Newbury (Son)	Carpenter (Estate)
No. 51 The Knapp	A. Newbury	Retired Farm Worker
	J. Newbury (Son)	Under Carter (Church Farm)

Horsefair

No. 52 The Knapp	T. Cleal	Under Cowman (Perry Farm)
	J. Cleal (Son)	Shop Worker (Walton's)
No. 53 The Knapp	J. Lane	Van Driver, Slaughterman (Bradley Stores)
No. 55 The Rank	E. Doman	Village Carrier & Coal Merchant
No. 56 The Rank	F. Doel	Head Painter (Estate)
	P. Doel (Son)	Under Carter (Estate)
	C. Doel (Son)	Estate Worker
No. 57 The Rank	A. Stone	Mason (Estate)
	E. Stone (Son)	Mason (Estate)
	F. Stone (Son)	Traveller for Lever Bros.
	J. Stone (Son)	Shop Worker (Walton's)
	D. Stone (Daughter)	Shop Worker (Walton's)
No. 58 The Rank	H. Miles	Spar Maker

	E. Miles (Son)	Gardener (Bradley House)
No. 59 The Rank	Miss Prowse	Retired
No. 60 The Rank	E. Smith	Plumber (Estate)
No. 61 The Rank	J. White	Gardener (Bradley House)
No. 62 The Rank	B. Whitty	Carpenter (E.J. Baker)
No. 63 The Rank	Shepp Ladd	Shepherd (Rodmead Farm)
No. 64 The Rank	F. Newbury	Sawmill Worker (Estate)
	L. Newbury (Son)	Farm Worker (Rodmead Farm)
	P. Newbury (Son)	Farm Worker (Perry Farm)
No. 65 The Rank	F. Elliott	Farm Worker (Church Farm)
No. 66 The Rank	W. Bailey	Farm Worker (Church Farm)
	W. White (Lodger)	Farm Worker (Church Farm)

High Street

School House	A.J. Scanes	Headmaster (Bradley School)
	E. Scanes (Son)	Gardener (Bradley House)
No. 67	Reading Room	
No. 68	P. Dryton	Retired
No. 70	Mrs. Howell	This house was used as a Laundry
	A. Howell (Daughter)	Helper in Laundry
	I. Howell (Daughter)	Helper in Laundry
No. 71	Mrs Gillanders	Widow of Head Forester (Estate)
	M. Gillanders (Daughter)	Village Nurse
	N. Gillanders (Daughter)	School Teacher
No. 72	W. Seaford	Head Butler (Bradley House)
No. 73	Miss Garrett	Caretaker Village Hall & School
No. 74	P.C. Attwell	Village Policeman
No. 75	E. Dennis	Carpenter (Estate)
No. 77	F. Doman	Worked for G. Locke
	C. Doman (Son)	Farm Worker (Perry Farm)
No. 78	C. Inman	Farm Worker (Newmead Farm)
No. 79	C. Merritt	Farm Worker (Perry Farm)
No. 80	J. Coleman	Farm Worker (Newmead Farm)
Grosvenor Square (Nos.81-85)		
	W. Alford	Blacksmith (H.J. Baker)
	H. Ludlow	Gardener (Bradley House)
	Mrs. Ludlow	Teacher (Bradley School)
	S. Tuffin	Cowman (to Duke of Somerset)
	J. Dowling	Retired
	S. Pothecary	Carter (Newmead Farm)
	I. Winchcombe	Blacksmith (H.J. Baker)
Perry Farm	R. Luff	Farmer

Dairy Farm	A. Wilson	Farmer
Baycliffe Farm	J. Crees	Farmer
	C. Crees (Son)	Farmer
Cottage No. 1	C. Waters	Farm Worker (Baycliffe)
Cottage No. 2	T. Gunter	Farm Worker (Baycliffe)

Frome Road

No. 86	F. White	Forestry Foreman (Estate)
No. 87	A. White	Farm Worker (Perry Farm)
	H. White (Son)	Farm Worker (Priory Farm)
	H. White (Son)	Farm Worker (Katesbench Farm)
No. 88	F. Waters	Sawmill Worker (Estate Sawmill)
No. 89	G. Trimby	Laurel Farm (Farm Manager)
	B.C. Leather	Worker for E. Doman
No. 90	E. Viney	Works for G. Locke
No. 91	W. White	Farm Worker (Church Farm)
No. 92	F. Mounty	Shepherd (Church Farm)
No. 93	S. Newbury	Farm Worker (Church Farm)
	L. Newbury (Son)	Farm Worker (Church Farm)
	M. Newbury (Son)	Farm Worker (Church Farm)
No. 94	J. Hacker	Postman (Bradley Post Office)
No. 95 (Trow Lane)	Mrs. White	Widow
	B. White (Son)	Farm Worker (Priory Farm)
No. 96 (Dunkerton)	W. Twin	Working in London
No. 97 do.	T. Ball	Forestry Worker (E. Doman)
No. 98 do.	F. Ball	Forestry Worker (G. Locke)
No. 99	H. Viney	Cleaner & Cellar Hand (Somerset Arms)
No. 100	I. Viney	Forestry Worker (G. Locke)
Katesbench Farm	B. Crees	Farmer
Mill Pond Cottages		
No. 101	S. Barge	Farm Worker (Priory Farm)
No. 102	" "	
	G. Dulake	Head Keeper (Estate)
Priory Farm	C. Court	Farmer
	A. Court (Son)	Working on farm
	H. Court (Son)	Working on farm
Keeper's Cottage (No.103)		Gamekeeper (Estate)

Manor of Yarnfield

Grange Farm	T. Ayles	Farmer
	S. Ayles (Son)	Farmer

	K. Ayles (Son)	Farmer
	H. Ayles (Son)	Farmer
Billishole Bottom	T. Murray	Farm Worker
Manor Farm	A.G. Lester	Farmer
	H. Lester (Son)	Farmer
Yarnfield Cottages	W. Guy	Roadman
	A. Newbury	Roadman
	Mrs. S. Chard	Widow
	Miss Chard (Daughter)	Domestic Worker
Yarnfield Bottom	Mrs. Selway	
	H. Hobbs	Farm Worker (Grange Farm)
Gare Hill		
Keeper's Cottage	S.Blackband	Gamekeeper (Estate)

On into the late 1920s

B Y THE MID 1920S many changes had taken place in the village. The Griffens, who ran the Post Office and the garage, had emigrated to Australia. Mr. and Mrs. George Beck came from Nunney and took over the Post Office. Alf and Max Griffen sold the garage business to Len Newbury (my cousin) who lived with his parents at number 50 on The Knapp. Since he came out of the army after serving in the 1914-18 war (involved with motor transport) he had been working in the Warminster Motor Co. garage where he gained experience in the repair of motor cars and motorcycles. He made the journey to Warminster daily on a Raleigh motorcycle.

Len Newbury soon built up a good business in the motor trade; in addition to repairing cars and motorbikes he sold new bicycles and stocked cycle spares. A few people in the village now had wireless sets so he also stocked wireless batteries as well as installing a plant for charging up the wireless accumulators. The wireless sets of the twenties needed two dry batteries (high tension and a grid bias) as well as an accumulator that needed a weekly charge.

Len Newbury also did local taxi work – first using an Arrol Johnson four-seater car but soon exchanging it for a Studebaker seven-seater limousine. Taxi work was on the increase and it was not very long before his brother Maurice left his job on the estate to go into partnership with him. Within a few years they had a petrol pump installed in the corner of the Knapp in front of the Post Office, and as cars became more popular they did a good trade in Shell petrol. They also had a Castrol oil cabinet on the Knapp for which there was a big demand as cars at this time used quite an amount of lubricating oil.

Len Newbury's expertise in repairing and servicing cars became well known around the district and he had as much work as he could manage.

The School

JOHN SCANES who had been Headmaster since the early 1900s retired. The family moved back to Ide but kept in touch with Maiden Bradley for a number of years by paying visits to the flower show and the church fete.

After having a temporary teacher at the school for some months a new Headmaster was appointed. He was Mr. P.F. Elderkin whose wife was also qualified, and as Mrs. Ludlow too had retired, Mrs. Elderkin took her place. Miss Nellie Gillanders left the school on her marriage to Basil Leather on Shrove Tuesday 1926; her job as infant teacher was taken by Mrs. Hilda Gray who travelled daily from Mere on an 'Ivy' motorcycle. Hilda later married Len Newbury.

In 1925 Kingston Deverill school was getting overcrowded and as Bradley school had room for up to thirty more children the Wiltshire County Council decided to send the 11 to 14 year olds from the Deverills to Maiden Bradley. Up to twenty children travelled each day from Monkton and Kingston Deverill by Basil Leather's bus under a contract that continued until 1930. Bradley school was now thriving again and full for a few years.

The Blacksmith, Wheelwright and Undertaker Business

THIS WAS ANOTHER BUSINESS in the village to change hands. Mr. H.J. Baker who had been the owner of the business for over 20 years retired and Mr. R.M. Duret became the new proprietor. On taking over he advertised locally that in addition to the existing business he would also be doing car repairs and sales as well as selling 'Pratts' petrol in two-gallon cans. He seemed to have ambitious plans for the car repair business but Len Newbury, now well established, did most of the car repairs needed in the village.

After a few years Mr. Duret set up in the building trade by buying a small lorry and employing a mason and labourer. So with the carpenters he already had he was able to do small building jobs in the surrounding district. The blacksmith's business was flourishing – all the farmers still had lots of horses to be shod and farming implements to be repaired.

When Mr.Duret came to the village he had a motorcycle combination called a 'Red Indian' and for a while he sold Red Indian motorbikes. He seemed to be full of ideas, always trying out something new. He had a fascination for Bean cars (very popular in the twenties) and in addition to one for his own use he sold quite a few to local farmers for use in the haymaking fields. An attachment was made by his blacksmith to fit a hay sweep to the front axle – he thought they had stronger front axles and were sturdier than a lot of other makes.

Mr. and Mrs. Duret joined in with most of the village activities; Mr. Duret played cricket for the local team and was a very good medium fast bowler.

The Estate Land Agent

MR. RUSSELL TAYLOR retired as the Duke of Somerset's agent and his place was taken by Major Walter L. Barton who with his family was now living at the 'Cottage'. He employed four servants in the house and a gardener/handyman who kept the household supplied with vegetables, in addition to keeping the huge garden and all the lawns in tip-top condition.

Mrs.Barton soon became involved in village affairs as did Major Barton who was chairman (and founder member) of the Maiden Bradley British Legion. He was chairman of both the village hall and flower show committees.

The Estate Forestry Department

MR. ALEXANDER MILNE was appointed Head Forester on the estate to replace Mr. A.J. Gillanders who had lived at the surgery in High Street with his wife and two daughters Nellie (school teacher) and Mary (village nurse). In July 1916 Mr. Gillanders had been to Oxford University to make arrangements for work on the Diploma Examination and while waiting at Oxford Station to catch the train back home he had a heart attack and died. He was only fifty seven years old and had moved here from Alnwick in April 1915. He was a prominent member of the forestry profession and author of a text book on forest insects. The Duke allowed Mrs.Gillanders and the two daughters to remain at the Surgery.

When Mr.Milne and family came to the village they lived at the Square. He was a good forester and kept the estate woodlands in first class condition. He remained in the job for nearly 20 years until his retirement but was still involved with the woods and other forestry work when he died in 1955 aged 81. He was appointed M.B.E. for services to forestry the year before he died. For the first few years the estate provided a motorised cycle for Mr. Milne to travel around the woods but eventually the rough roads proved too much for the bike so he had to revert to pony and trap.

Walton's Stores

MR. JOSEPH GIBBONS, the manager of the local shop, who had been in the village since the early 1900s also decided it was time to retire. He had two daughters who had both worked in the shop, one in the office and the other in the drapery department. The family moved to Frome and the two daughters were married to Frome businessmen and spent their whole married lives in the town.

The new manager of Walton's was Mr. Frank Phelps who turned out to be a very efficient man for the job. Mr. Phelps had a family of six children – three boys and three girls – one of whom worked in the shop in charge of the office department. Mr. Phelps had a Morris car in which he travelled around the villages taking orders (like his predecessor) that were subsequently delivered by the shop vans. He continued to employ a boy during school holidays to help in the 'business room'. This was one of the big rooms at the rear of the shop where bulk commodities were stored such as sugar and tea. All this had to be weighed up into small amounts, one pound and two pound bags.

Doctor Pope Bartlett

DR. BARTLETT who had been the village doctor for more than 20 years also retired. He had been a very loyal and respected servant and friend to the village. My parents told me that Dr. Bartlett would always turn out whatever the weather or time of night if someone was ill. He was keen on photography and took many pictures around the village – the most popular was 'Chip Cottage', home of Grace White. The house was situated just inside the woods at the junction of the Bruton Road and the lane going to Gare Hill, but although a pretty little cottage it was very isolated and had no internal water. This had to be fetched from a spring nearly a quarter of a mile down the hill in the wood – a laborious task having to struggle up the hill with buckets of water.

Grace White, had been living in the cottage alone and when she died the estate had the house pulled down. The boundary hedge and garden gate together with gooseberry bushes and other shrubs remained intact for a number of years. Dr. Bartlett sold lots of photographs of Chip Cottage and most of the village people bought a copy.

Dr. G. E. Ellis took over the practice from Dr. Bartlett. He was a younger man with more modern ideas and qualifications and soon gained the respect of the village people. He remained at the practice for many years until his retirement around 1960.

Village Life

I T S E E M E D that so many business people who had been in the village since the early 1900s had by the mid 1920s decided to retire, but life in the village carried on much about the same. When the boys left school they would either go to work on the estate or on farms and there was never a problem finding a job. The girls would go into service – Bradley House and the Cottage still employed a lot of servants and so did most of the farmers – but some would have to leave home to do so. The wages were so low that all the big houses could afford to keep quite a large staff.

There were two most welcome business changes. We were now having milk brought around to our houses daily, something that had never been done before. Bert Smith carried two buckets of milk (hanging on chains from yokes on his shoulders) around the village door to door measuring out the milk into people's jugs. For most people a morning delivery was sufficient but Bert would call again in the afternoon if required. His customers could now order a rabbit from him on his rounds for sixpence each.

The other welcome change was Leather's carrier's business which changed from horse transport to motor transport in 1923 as mentioned earlier.

People soon became accustomed to this form of transport and it became well patronised – the Wednesday trip to Frome Market was very popular and services were also run (on alternate Saturdays) to Warminster and Frome for shopping. There was a service to Frome on Saturday evenings for the pictures although most of the shops stayed open until 8 pm and the market stalls were busy selling fruit and vegetables and other things until around 9 pm. People would hang around the stalls waiting for a bargain; when it was time for the traders to pack up they would sell off their stock very cheaply rather than have to take it back home – you could often buy a big bag of fruit for a shilling!

Basil Leather kept the carrier's service with the pony and wagon going to Warminster on alternate Saturdays until 1927/28 when old Tommy the pony was pensioned off. All journeys were now taken by motor transport which included trips to the seaside in the summer, a service well patronised. Basil bought a money bag, a whistle and a pocket book and set me up as a conductor, when I was twelve years of age, on the Saturday service and during school holidays. I would ride in the back of the bus but when it was full I would stand on the steps outside and give a blast on the whistle when passengers got on or off. We did not have tickets, so I used to record the passengers' names in the pocket book! I was now spending most of my spare time in Basil Leather's yard.

I had won a scholarship to Warminster Technical College but my mother thought it would be difficult to find the money to keep me at school until I

Maiden Bradley Women's Institute outing in 1925, photographed at Weymouth Coach Park

reached the age of 16. I had therefore to forgo the scholarship and set my sights on finding a job when I left school at the age of 14. There was no school transport provided at the time except that the Education Authority would have lent me a bicycle to do the journey to Warminster. At the end of my school days the bike would have had to be returned in good condition but they were willing to pay fourpence (2p) per week for its maintenance.

My father was earning thirty shillings a week (£1.50) at the time and mother had her elderly father living with us – his only income was ten shillings a week old age pension – so they did not think it was such a hardship for me to start earning my keep at the age of fourteen. I remember at the time my schoolmaster was not very pleased that we turned the scholarship down as he thought that I would have found a much better job had I gone on to the Grammar School. In the 1920s there were not many working-class families that could afford to send their children on to the Grammar School.

Father earned quite a nice bit of overtime each summer for a number of years working at Priory Farm for Mr. C. Court helping with the haymaking. By the mid twenties he had changed his job. He had left the estate forestry department (where he had been earning thirty shillings a week) to work for the Wiltshire County Council as a roadman. He had a 10% increase when his wage rose to thirty-three shillings a week! I remember mother saying the extra three shillings would be enough to buy a joint of meat for Sunday lunch (a good joint of meat could be bought for that in those days). Father, as well as having a garden adjoining the house, also cultivated two allotments, so we were usually well supplied with an array of vegetables for most of the year.

One advantage of living in Maiden Bradley in the 1920s was the cheap house rents. We lived at 49 Church Street and mother paid two shillings and fivepence per week (12p now) rent which included rates and a good supply of water. The estate kept the outside in good repair and regularly painted. It was father's responsibility to keep the inside in good order.

Between the end of World War I and the mid 1920s two of the village farms changed hands. Mr. A.R. Gifford left Rodmead Farm and moved to a farm at Colerne and Mr.Rawlins who had been farming at Horton near Devizes took over. From Priory Farm Mr. C. Court moved to Whatley and Mr. H. Cottell moved in.

Some of the farmers who had previously been taking their milk to the Staplemead milk factory by horse transport had now changed to more modern methods. Mr. Beak of Newmead Farm bought a new lorry (a 'Garford') and took his milk, as well as that of two other farms, to the milk factory daily. Mr. J. Ayles of Grange Farm also bought a new Model T. Ford lorry and took his milk to Gillingham Station daily where it was taken to London by train.

By the mid 1920s Mr. James D. Beak of Newmead Farm was well-known throughout the country for his herd of pedigree Gloucester Old Spot pigs and he regularly took prizes at most of the agricultural shows in the West Country as well as some in the Midlands. He won many championships and was known as one of the top breeders in England.

Basil Leather was also getting his name in the local papers for winning prizes with his poultry. His most popular breed was Indian Game with which he had numerous winners, including many cups and championships at shows as far afield as London, Birmingham and Wales.

There was no shortage of musical talent in the local villages, although there now was no brass or silver band in Maiden Bradley. We did however have a string orchestra under the direction of Mr. Bert Ludlow who carried out many engagements in the hall on winter evenings.

Our nearest band was Zeals Silver Band who usually carried out the Bradley engagements. Basil Leather had the contract to transport them on all their bookings and the longest trip they ever went on was to London to the Crystal Palace band contest. What a journey in a Ford Model T! They left Zeals at 6 am and got home at 6 am the following day – not too bad I suppose seeing that the speed limit was then twelve miles per hour.

Basil Leather was a very keen track athlete. He was champion for many miles around for distances from 100 yards to one mile and his prizes included silver mounted ebony walking sticks, shields and silver cigarette cases. Wherever he ran at sports events in the district he was known for winning and was usually handicapped – in the mile race he generally had to start a hundred yards behind the other competitors but even then he would usually win. Ray Newbury (my cousin) was champion high jumper in the district; he had many trophies and was well known for his high jumping skills.

Basil Leather was looked upon as a kingpin of village life. He had a hand in helping to organise most events that took place including whist drives, dances, socials and concerts – he had a good singing voice and performed at most of these.

The dances were held in the Village Hall during the winter months and there were plenty of good dance bands to be had. A couple of the best were Stan Beacham's Orchestra (five piece) from Frome or Les Whitmarsh's Orchestra from Warminster (four or five piece). They started at 8 pm and finished at 2 am with an interval of approximately an hour for refreshments. They were usually very popular and quite an amount of money was handed over to local charities. Sometimes, to cater for all ages, they would organise a whist drive and dance – whist from 7.30 till 10 pm and then dancing from 10.15 to 2 am.

For 'Men Only' Basil would, at least once a year, organise a charabanc outing to either Weston-Super-Mare or Weymouth – again a very popular day out. Refreshments were taken like bread, cheese, pickles and tomatoes as well as a few jars of beer and other liquid refreshments. A stop was made on route for an hour or more, usually if going to Weston it was made in Cheddar Gorge or if the outing was to Weymouth at Cerne Abbas (The Giant's Head).

Maiden Bradley Frothblowers outing to Weston-super-Mare, 1930, including Arthur Newbury (the bones), Frank Ball (Accordion) and Harry Viney (Concertina).

In addition to refreshments there were always musicians on board to provide music for a sing-song with a few talented older men bringing along their instruments. Frank Ball and Arthur Newbury were experts on the accordion, Harry Viney on the concertina, Ted Viney on the mouth organ and others with 'the bones' and tambourines. I remember one occasion, when jars of beer were being hoisted on to a rock in Cheddar Gorge, refreshments being handed around and music being played, that attracted quite a number of spectators from other charabanc parties parked nearby. They stood around and listened to the music and all clapped when the musicians had performed!

When the charabancs arrived at the seaside parking place there was always a photographer with his camera and tripod waiting to take a picture of the party before they got out. They would find out the time of leaving for home and they would be waiting in the parking place with lots of photographs hoping to sell them to the passengers before they left. This outing for men was always very popular and Basil never had any difficulty finding enough passengers – it became known as the Frothblowers outing and continued for a number of years.

Basil Leather, just arrived at Weymouth with the Chevrolet Charabanc.
Bessie Ford, Bert Newbury, Mrs. F. Newbury, Frank Bealing, Luie Beale,
Mrs. F. Seal, Bob Seal, Jack Seal, Mrs. Biffen, Brenda Newbury, Mrs. B. Newbury,
Bill Newbury, Mrs. Lane, Fred Lane, Percy Dulake and Don Newbury

In 1925 I still had to do two more years at school and I remember during the Easter holidays Basil said he had to go to London to fetch a load of furniture for the vicar, the Reverend Wilcox, and would I like to go with him. Well, I jumped at the opportunity of a trip to London (not many folk in the village had ever been there). The plan was to leave Bradley at 9 am in order to meet Basil's friend at 6 pm at Kew Bridge who would then show us the way through London to his house at Haringey. Here we would spend the night before going on next morning to pick up the load of furniture at W. J. Jelks warehouse at Southgate returning home the same day. Things did not work out quite as planned because the day before we were due to go the lorry developed 'back axle trouble'. Basil took it to the Ford dealers (Scotts of Frome) for repairs which took longer than expected and we therefore did not set out on our trip to London until 4 pm –

instead of 9 am. Consequently we arrived at Kew Bridge at 10 pm with no sign of Basil's friend waiting to escort us through London. After waiting for a while Basil decided to find his own way to Pemberton Road, Haringey, in North London where his friend lived. After another couple of hours and half dozen cups of coffee at the all night stalls we eventually arrived at our destination where we were welcomed by the friend's wife but there was no sign of Harry. He arrived soon after us explaining that he had been noticed by the Police hanging around on Kew Bridge for such a long time that they had taken him in for questioning and it was some while before they would let him go.

We went over to Southgate next morning, got the lorry loaded and started our journey home about midday – the lorry was heavily laden and I could see that we were going to have a hard journey home. After a lot of enquiries we eventually found our way back through London on the road to the West and we got back as far as Bagshot before we needed to fill up with petrol. The old lorry had been getting hot and not pulling very well so Basil asked the old man at the garage if he would find out what was wrong. He spent some time checking things over and after a trial run up the hill we were again on our way home hoping we would get home without further trouble. We eventually arrived back at Maiden Bradley at 10 pm without any further breakdowns and after a good night's sleep we unloaded the lorry. The vicar wanted it unpacked and spread out on the front lawn; it was amazing the amount of goods we brought back on the old Ford Model T!

With the exception of going to London with Zeals Band this was the only time Basil undertook such a long journey with the old Ford.

I was getting to the end of my school days and as the time was drawing near my mother kept asking me what I was going to do when I left school – had Basil offered me a job? Actually Basil had never mentioned anything about a job, so I was not sure what I was going to do. Mother said 'you had better ask him if he wants you to work for him' but I still did not say anything to him.

When school broke up in July 1927 for the summer holidays I went round in the yard as usual on the Friday afternoon. I said to Basil that I had left school and before I had a chance to say anything more he said 'Oh good, when are you going to start – Monday morning?' I said I would like to have a week's holiday and start work on Monday week. I asked 'What are you going to pay me?' and he replied, 'Eight shillings (40p) a week, Monday to Friday 8 am to 5 pm and Saturday 8 am till 12.30 pm'. He also said 'Your first job every morning is to clean out the stables. After you have done that you will have your orders for the rest of the day.'

After a few weeks my work day was extended, I started at 7 am and finished anything from 5.30 pm (quite often we did not arrive home until 6 or 6.30 pm). Basil had taken on a contract from Bradley Estate to haul two hundred tons of larch timber from Wallace (near Gare Hill) to Witham Station. The timber was cut in 6 ft lengths to be used as pit props and the hardest part of the contract was loading it into the railway trucks which were higher than our wagons. Most of the hauling was done by horse transport but on the odd occasion the lorry would take a few loads.

I really got fed up with going to work that first winter. We were leaving home at 7 am in the dark and not getting home till 5 or 6 pm in the dark again. I shall always remember those days, often getting wet through in the morning and having to stay in wet clothes all day. However, in the spring of 1928 the Witham contract was finished and I was doing more varied work. I was sometimes lorry driver's mate and sometimes working with the horse on county council road work.

The road tarring season started in the early spring and would last for eight to twelve weeks. The council would need three horses for this; one to pull the tarring machine and two horses with carts for laying gravel. The chap with the tar machine (pot) horse would have to help pump the boiling tar out of the pot to a man wearing special overalls and a veil over his face, who would spray it on to the road. It was reckoned in good weather to do one mile of road per week. Most years we would do the B3092 from the Somerset boundary at the bottom of Bradley Hill to the A303 at Zeals (bottom of Bells Lane) a distance of six miles and this was usually done in six weeks. Basil sent me with the tar pot horse as it was supposed to be the easiest job.

The Wiltshire County Road Surveyor, Capt. Filor of Mere, would pay a visit to the tar spraying gang at least once a week to make sure everything was OK. I used to keep out of sight when he was around but on one occasion, within my first month on the job, he noticed me and asked the ganger called Harry Antill what the boy was doing. Harry said he was with the Leather's tar pot horse. He told him to go over to Maiden Bradley and tell Leather to send a man with the horse as the council paid for a man and a horse. So I did not go again for a few weeks but eventually he sent me back and sure enough on my first day with the horse Capt. Filor saw me. He had another go at the ganger and asked me how much Mr. Leather paid me. I said, 'Eight shillings a week Sir'. Harry Antill told him I was a good chap and was quite capable of working as well as a man so Capt. Filor said that if Mr. Leather would pay me a man's wage then he had no objection to me staying on the job. My wages were increased to ten shillings a week (50p now) – I didn't get the 'man's pay' but that seemed to be the end of the affair and I was now the permanent 'tar pot boy!'

When there was no council work we worked in the woods. I soon learned the skills of the timber trade which was again very hard work – no chain saws but only crosscut saws, hatchets and bill hooks. Basil bought most of his timber from the Duke's estate but sometimes from Stourhead or Longleat. Either we thinned fir plantations or bought heads of trees for firewood (usually oak or ash) as well as parcels of underwood from which we turned out faggots, poles for fencing and pea and bean sticks.

I remember that within the first few weeks of starting work I was persuaded to become a bellringer by one of my work mates, Harold White (the carter). He said that they were trying to recruit another six or more lads to learn bellringing and would be having practice at least one evening each week when tuition would be available. I found this to be a good evening's recreation and by Christmas 1927 we were qualified to ring on Christmas morning at 6 am, as was the custom. We also rang the Old Year out and the New Year in.

In those days on winter evenings you climbed the steps to the ringing chamber with the aid of a flash lamp. The chamber was lit by two little oil lamps which gave just about enough light for us to read the numbers on the ringing sheets.

In the winter of 1927/28 we had some severe weather. The snow started on Boxing Day and by the following morning Maiden Bradley was completely cut off – all roads blocked by drifts up to six feet deep – and it was some days before traders were able to reach us. At the time there was no mechanical means of clearing the snow so it was done by manual labour.

Fortunately the telephone wires were still intact so outside communication was not affected. The Wiltshire County Council phoned Basil Leather and authorised him to recruit labour to get the roads open in the district. He soon had a gang of eight or ten men who arrived with shovels ready to start digging a track wide enough to allow a vehicle to get through. Priority was given to the B3092 and next the road from Bradley to Warminster but it was some eight or nine days before the Yarnfield Road was open.

Gangs from Mere and Warminster were digging a track towards Maiden Bradley and eventually all roads were open – it was frustrating, however, as the strong winds would blow the snow off the fields and block the roads again. The horse-drawn snow plough was brought into action to keep the roads clear.

The horses were often needed by the council during the winter to help the steam roller gang repairing roads – one horse with the water barrel and two horses with carts for hauling the stone. My job was to keep the steam roller supplied with water and to water in the stone.

By the winter of 1929 both Percy Snook and I had reached the age of 16 and were now old enough to become members of the Maiden Bradley Reading Room, to which we were duly elected. We soon learned all the games and after a couple of years were able to hold our own with the rest of the lads.

As we came to the end of the 1920s the postal service in the area was completely rearranged. Our postal address was now Maiden Bradley, Warminster, Wiltshire. The Maiden Bradley sorting office was closed and the mail handled by Warminster, so our postmen all retired – Jim Hacker, George Howell and Charlie Newbury. Ernie Newbury continued the Maiden Bradley delivery for a time before he also retired. The Deverills' mail was now delivered by the Warminster postmen as well as Norton Ferris and Kilmington. The Gare Hill and Witham Friary deliveries were carried out by Frome staff. With Ernie Newbury's retirement the Bradley mail was handled entirely by Warminster.

Not many improvements in living standards had taken place during the past decade. The average labourer's wage was still around thirty shillings per week. Cooking and heating water were still being done on the open fire grates although some people had started to buy Valor oil stoves for cooking. These were quite useful as they saved lighting up the fire in summer weather. A few more cottages had been connected to the main sewer and there were more tradesmen from the towns calling to sell their wares. There was even a dentist from Frome (Mr. Crouch) who came to the village on Monday evenings, and one could go along to the surgery and have a tooth taken out for two shillings without an appointment.

Just before Christmas each year Basil had the contract to deliver 'Charity Coal' to the pensioners, widows and widowers of the parish. A sum of money had been left in trust to pay for three hundredweight of coal each year for the poor and needy of Maiden Bradley as a Christmas gift which was very much appreciated by all who received it.

Throughout the 1920s Walton's bakery in the village was kept very busy. As well as supplying the village with bread and cakes they also supplied Gare Hill, Witham Friary and some of the other surrounding villages. The bakehouse as it was known locally, was at the rear of 43 Church Street where the baker, Johnny Elsworth, lived. His busiest time of the year was at Easter and Christmas. At Easter when the shop usually took orders for more than 1,000 hot cross buns my father, who in his younger days had been a baker, would go on the Thursday night before Good Friday to help make them. He would go at 7 pm and work all night till about 6 am on Good Friday morning. I used to go and lend a hand – weigh up the dough and put the crosses on the buns – and Basil would also come and help. We used to have a break about every three hours when Johnny would make a cup of tea. We would get the buns bagged up ready to load on to the delivery van by 7 am when many were still hot.

Another busy time for the baker was at Christmas when Walton's would take orders for cakes and other fare as well as offering a service to cook the Christmas joint or bake the cake. A lot of people would rather pay sixpence than risk cooking their Christmas joint or cake on their open grate which was often very unreliable.

The Beginning of the End

THERE WERE LONG PERIODS during the 1920s when all the working population had employment within the parish. The biggest single employer was the estate who employed masons, carpenters, painters, plumbers, sawmill workers, timber hauliers and forestry workers. There were usually up to eight men employed in Bradley House gardens and another three or four in the stables, as well as chauffeurs and handymen. There was one period when Church Farm employed fourteen men and one school leaver in addition to the three farm bosses, Alfred Jeffries and his two sons Harry and Charlie. Included in the total were seven Newburys from four different families in the village.

As the twenties were drawing to a close some of the younger workers were getting dissatisfied with village wages, as much more could be earned by working in town. Two of the estate carpenters (who had been with them since leaving school) left and got jobs at Westlands – Ray Newbury and Charlie Seal each bought a motorbike and travelled to Yeovil to work. Eddy Stone, one of the young estate masons, went to work at Frome for Barnes the Builders. They were all now earning much more than estate workers but the older men seemed happy enough and continued to stay in Maiden Bradley and work at the local rates of pay.

Editor's Postscript

T HESE ARE DON'S RECOLLECTIONS of how life in Maiden Bradley changed between the wars almost exactly as he has recounted them to his granddaughter, Margaret Cooper. The editors have made the minimum of alterations in the hope that his story of village life in those far-off days emerges from these pages as vividly as when he tells it himself.

Chris Oliver
James Clark
February 2004

Index

This is a selective index of persons, places and subjects. It omits the directory section, pages 53-8, and names in group captions.

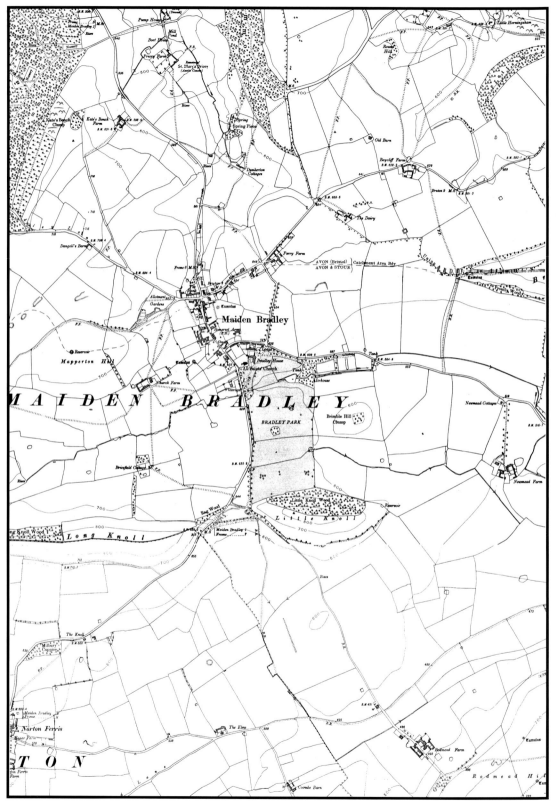

Ordnance Survey 6-inch scale plan, revised in 1923 (reduced to 3 inches = 1 mile)